Confessions of a Neglected African Daughter

Kwasi Bosompem

with Best wishes

Kwasi Bosompem

May 30, 1992

PRDC Publishing
Silver Spring, Maryland

Confessions of a Neglected African Daughter

Acknowledgments
Special thanks to Maxine Brown-Roberts and Sara
Simmons for their comments and assistance, and Remel
Quaye and Wizzy for the illustrations.
- KB

Library of Congress
Cataloging in Publication Data
ISBN 0-9649351-1-2: $9.60

Published by
PRDC Publishing
P. O. Box 3369
Woodmoor Branch
Silver Spring, Maryland 20918

Printed in the United States of America
by M&T Printing, Fairfax, Virginia

Dedicated to my children, Rodney and Daphne,
who kept me strong during the long days and hours
it took to write this story.

CHAPTER 1
Home Sweet Home Not !

March 1987

Beyond the banks of River Birim, in the eastern woodlands of Ghana, lies the town of Akim Oda, the traditional and administrative seat of the Kotoku people. The terrain of Akim Oda is undulating, and the tropical forests are full of fruits and food. Although the land has been cultivated over the years, the soils are as fertile as ever. Semi-commercial agricultural production and food exported from its hinterland support the population. Timber, minerals, and the produce from the rich forests account for the resources of the land. Diamonds and gold are also plentiful in the vast Akim territory. The precious diamonds of the world are dredged along the banks of the river, while foreign companies mine the gold. Farmers in the area have been digging and tilling the land for years. As such, the town flourished within a short period. The basic occupations in the area are mining and farming. However, Akim Oda has also produced professionals, including doctors, lawyers, and teachers.

Since most of these professionals work outside the town and in foreign countries, their constant remittances home, as well as vacations to the homeland, have motivated most youth, including a teenager by the name of Akosua Sojourner Mensah. A student in the local high school, Akosua was determined to have a future and be like the number of professionals who regularly came on vacation.

1

That was her ambition. Every weekend, the local bus station became the main activity center as families bid farewell to their sons and daughters returning to their places of employment away from Akim Oda. There were always homecoming celebrations, and the local restaurant and bar at the local bus terminal was always hectic. Families, relatives, friends, and lovers gathered to listen to music while awaiting the arrival or departure of loved ones.

Akim Oda itself, was a sprawling African town, being cosmopolitan in population. It is composed of an old town separated by a railway from the commercially and residentially mixed new town. Tribes and clans lived in a mixed area separated from commercial and business activities.

Mr. John Mensah, the head of the Mensah household, had five customary wives serving him as a king in the town. They included Mrs. Joanne Mensah, the first wife, who was also Akosua's mother. However, the probability of Mr. Mensah's marriage to a new-found love during a business trip was always very high. They all lived in a large compound house with a three-story mansion attached. The compound was about sixty by fifty meters in area. Each wife lived in a condominium unit, with a bath. There were five kitchens and two other main baths and toilets for the rest of the household. The old man himself lived on the third floor of the mansion. The young women and the boys, whose mothers were not on the premises, lived on the second and the third floors respectively.

Over the years, Mr. Mensah had not stopped his love pursuits and polygamous life. It was not possible to count all the children in the house. When all the children gathered in the evenings, the noise was terrible. The total household on such noisy evenings included neighbors and friends, and at times the numbers could not be estimated. There were times when, Akosua could not remember exactly the total household numbers, especially the young women. There was always a different face in the house, and she never knew who Mr. Mensah's latest fiancee was or who were her half sisters, some of whom she had never met. Despite his large family in those years, Mr. Mensah was still having babies.

The daily order in the house never changed. Early in the morning, each person had their duties. Some fetched water from either the public taps or the River Birim, others swept the compound, while the strong lads vacuumed the rooms, and cleaned the floors, tables, and other furniture in the living room. It was trouble for a child in the household to refuse to do his or her duties. That person would receive punishment from Mr. Mensah. Roll call was regular, and inspection of work was strict.

Meals were a problem, at times, for the boys with no mothers around. Those with their mothers in the house were always assured of a second round of food to eat in their mother's kitchen. The boys, especially those who had no mothers around, suffered the most. They had to stay around and be attentive to the bell of Mr. Mensah, signaling he had finished eating. The person closest to the dining room then had to run to collect the leftovers and carry the food to the ground floor where all the boys would eat the food from the same bowl. At times, you could count about ten hands in a plate. They all ate with their fingers from the same dish. Some boys were always around; they could not afford to be late, let alone be absent.

Mr. Mensah kept a very strict discipline and forced lifestyle on Akosua and had sworn to make her an example to the others in everything. When she was eighteen, he forbade Akosua from entertaining friends, let alone having a boyfriend. He prevented all his daughters from dating men or even playing outside the home. One evening, as he relaxed in his special gold decorated chair and enjoyed the evening's blowing breeze, he placed his favorite drink near his chair and added some herbs. He took a sip and left the bottle under the chair. Mr. Mensah looked around the compound and shouted, "Akosua! Akosua!"

"Yes, Papa?" Akosua replied.

"All right, Akosua. I just called to ensure you were home."

Akosua was one of Mr. Mensah's most beautiful daughters. She had a dark complexion and was about five feet tall. She was very intelligent; however, the story at home was not bright for her. Mr. Mensah called her every minute. At times, he just called for no other reason than to make sure Akosua had not gone out. At other times, Akousa had her usual work to be done at home. He was not interested in the education of his children. As much as society allowed, he shirked his major social responsibility as a father. It was also common knowledge that Mr. Mensah would never allow his children to attend any higher institution or college. After one's basic high school education, even career training school was a hard sell. He would have preferred that everyone become a businessperson. Anything with immediate return on investments was more meaningful to him. His ideas and thoughts about colleges made it impossible to discuss any educational plans with him. Truly, Akosua did not remember any day she had ever had a serious conversation with him as a father. It was difficult because the man was always angry with someone or something. Mr. Mensah used to be a strong man who had worked hard for his wealth; however, he was getting older and poorer.

On another evening in the hot summer months as Mr. Mensah relaxed on a chair on the porch of his three-story mansion, he called Akosua again. "Akosua, Akosua!" shouted Mr. Mensah.

"Papa?" Akosua replied.

"Bring me a toothpick and a paper towel immediately. Hurry!" he ordered and continued, "I warn you, Akosua especially, and all of you in this house. At this time of year, it is not safe to be out in the night because of the traditional festivals in the town. I warn all of you, my daughters, not to go out at night. If anyone entertains a boyfriend and becomes pregnant before marriage, that person will be out of my household. Teenage pregnancy is what I hate most," he concluded. "Thank you," he said to Akosua as she brought the toothpick and the paper towel.

Akosua tried to study every evening for her High School Diploma Examinations, and she worried a lot about her future. She was not happy at home. It was affecting her studies. She realized that attending school was not interesting anymore. The senior citizens had seen the better life twenty years ago. There were even several signs of the past. There were no free lunches, no bananas, no rice, no fried plantain at noon. She even did manual labor around the school.

Imagine a teenager like Akosua Mensah cutting grass with a cutlass. In this modern age of technology, she could not believe herself cutting a lawn with a cutlass. She realized it had been years since the white man gave independence, packed up, and left the land of Ghana. But despite all the technological advancement, Akim-Oda High School could not even afford a mower to cut the lawns. As such, students were still doing manual labor. She thought it would destroy her natural beauty if she continued to cut grass and do manual work like that every day.

At school, her teachers were often absent, and she did not have a permanent teacher. Within the last year alone, five different teachers had come and left the school. Her school compound was not as it had been. All the date palm trees grown were dead. The lawns and gardens were in a poor state, as if they had never been maintained. Most of the flowers on the school campus had been destroyed.

Sanitation and basic infrastructure were major problems. The once beautiful natural landscape was no longer beautiful. Although the church community was as organized as ever, the old church building was in ruins. Money was hard to come by to make the needed repairs to the building. This problem was making church attendance very difficult for some Christians in the town. The church building could have collapsed at any time. The walls were cracked and the ceilings leaked. Water dripped from the ceiling during prayer sessions. Efforts of the once-good Christians and others were being hampered.

On the local economy, producer prices of raw materials had fallen low. They were worth nothing. Producer prices could not cope with inflationary trends. The dependence on one commercial crop without any diversification was a major problem. When the local economy failed to sustain itself, the farmer was disregarded in society. Mr. John Mensah could not be working for such low returns in semi-commercial farming. That was why he was a jack-of-all-trades, doing business, farming, buying and selling general merchandise, and stone contracting. He had lost money on most of his businesses.

Akosua never understood whether these economic hardships were the main reason for the actions of her father toward her. She never really understood the reasons why her father did not make life comfortable for her in the large household. Akosua was not happy at home. There was much pressure on her from her parents that she did not understand. She began to suspect the reason when her mother started discussing marriage affairs with her. It was a big shock for Akosua when her mother talked about all the nice things about marriage after school. Mrs. Mensah continued discussing marriage with Akosua at any opportune time, until Akosua realized her parents were arranging her marriage to an old rich farmer by the name of Papa James immediately after high school.

"Oh, Akosua," said her mother one evening, "you have to plan your future. At eighteen years, you are a young woman of age now. Some of your other friends have their marriages planned at your age. They marry the most respectable man they can find, settle down as homemakers while planning the birth of their babies. Some of your friends are even doing well in home business and raising their children. You have to plan your life and think of what to do after your examinations. We will help you find a respectable man to marry."

This annoyed Akosua, and she protested vehemently, "Why me?! Why me?! Please do not give me to anyone. I will plan my marriage when I am ready. In these modern times, young women of my age group do not believe in the old society and arranged marriages. You have made my life very difficult. You have separated me from others in town. You have blocked a thousand and one opportunities. And now, you are telling me what to do." She could not believe what her mother had told her. She ran to her room and slammed the door behind her.

Mr. Mensah immediately walked in and shouted, "What is happening? Akosua! Be careful! Akosua! Do not say that. It is not nice to speak to your mother in such language. You are a disrespectful, lazy, young person." Her father scolded her that evening. "This will be the first and last time you confront your mother in such harsh words," Mr. Mensah said. "After all, I can easily walk you out of the house, if necessary," he concluded. Mrs. Mensah also did not stop scolding and warning her.

Akosua had been indoors most of the time since this confrontation with her parents. She began to imagine several options of what to do with her life after school. She could not do anything without peace of mind, as well as moral and financial support. "What parents! They do not want to make life comfortable for me. It has been so difficult to study for my examinations and continue my education as others. There is always trouble in the house. I have to do something before it's too late," she said to herself.

Some minutes later, Mr. Mensah shouted again. "Akosua! Akosua!"

She did not respond this time, but thought to herself, "I might as well face this old man. I have a month before my final examinations, and I'll never have peace of mind."

"Akosua," continued Mr. Mensah. He asked one of the girls in the house to call Akosua from her room. It was definitely another attack on Akosua, although she did not know the reason for the call. However, she stood up and walked toward her father. The old man was very annoyed. Seeing her, he burst out, "You! Akosua, I warned and advised you to keep away from that student. I hear that you jump walls in the night and follow this boy."

Mr. Mensah was angry, but he was telling the truth. He was as furious as ever and wanted to flog Akosua with his big cane as she walked toward him. Immediately, Akosua knelt down and burst into tears. Mr. Mensah complained that he had heard many stories about Akosua and a boy in the neighborhood from his friends. Mr. Mensah refused to admit that Akosua had grown and matured. He shouted and scolded Akosua. It was difficult for her to explain her story to him, as he was not interested in any explanation. At eighteen, Akosua had grown and believed she could take care of herself. It was then she realized that all the pressures on her were due to the planned marriage Mr. and Mrs. Mensah had arranged for her after she finished school. The "boy" Mr. Mensah was referring to, was her high school sweetheart. Akosua had been going out with this boy named Essien for almost a year without Mr. Mensah's knowledge. The two were very close friends. However her father had recently been hearing reports from the neighbors and especially from the old farmer who wanted Akosua for marriage.

One Tuesday evening before the strict warning by Mr. Mensah, Akosua and Essien had gone to a concert. A concert group, the Star-Jokers, had come to the Premier Hotel at Akim Oda. Everyone was out in the night. Essien whistled for Akosua. The two had a special whistle greeting. Hearing the whistle, Akosua stole a duplicate key and sneaked out of the house to the concert with Essien.

Mr Mensah   Akosua

Mr. Mensah did not notice. Akosua did not know exactly who might have reported this to him. However, she enjoyed herself that night. People from every corner of the town came to the dance. The town was rocking to the music. The music of the band was loud. Akosua could not resist such an event. After all, her classmates preparing for the High School Diploma Examinations were present at the concert.

Essien had often been requesting Akosua to go to bed with him. No matter how many promises and requests she made to him to wait until after her final examinations, he would not listen. Akosua loved Essien but did not really initially believe in teenage premarital sex. That night after the Star Jokers concert, Essien tried to make love to Akosua. She resisted him with a struggle. It all happened near the football grounds on the route to her home. The two saw someone with a flashlight on the street. Essien then pushed Akosua down onto the grass and said quietly, "Get down! It may be your father carrying the flashlight. He must be returning home. He must have spent the evening in the house of the owner of the restaurant across the road," Essien speculated.

On the ground, Essien gave Akosua a good kiss after kisses. He held Akosua down with all the strength he had, then tried to force her to take her clothes off. Essien realized he was up to a tough fight. Akosua pushed Essien off. She stood up while Essien laid down, tired but pleading to make love to Akosua. It was a quiet, late night and the wind was blowing. There were still noises on the streets after the concert. Akosua then talked to Essien, promising him all the best she had if he could only wait until after her final examinations. As he still laid down tired, Akosua left him and went straight home. She knew if it were Mr. Mensah who passed by with the flashlight he might be looking for her.

Mr. Mensah was, however, at home still awake. He was looking down the street waiting for any of his children who went out in the night to come by. Akosua saw him from afar and hurriedly entered the house through the back door. It was not surprising that Mr. Mensah was so annoyed the following day.

Akosua, even at this age, had not been taught sex education at home or at school. It was even taboo to discuss sex in public during those times. All she knew was learned from stories by her classmates and other friends. She even found it difficult to believe some of them. The stories and gossip about love and relationships were a way to make them happy at school. Akosua even felt ashamed to talk to her friends at school about what Essien tried to do to her after the concert. They had warned her previously about the possibilities of Essien forcing her to have sex. She did not worry much that night because it was the second time Essien had tried to force her to have sex. In her mind she was more worried about all the problems at home than about Essien.

She was, however, filled with enjoyment at the concert. That night the Star Jokers did their most popular song called "Show Your Love". This was Akosua's favorite. She had memorized all the words. She was totally thrilled by the song. Up to this day she still sings their tunes.

The days after the concert were unbearable for Akosua. It was not that different from other normal days, except there was a closer watch on her. Mr. Mensah kept shouting and complaining about Essien. There was a continued attempt to stop Akosua from going out with him. Any time she attempted to study, there would be a call from her parents. There was also the same routine in the house as always. Either the toilet must be cleaned, dishes washed, or laundry done. There was always work in the household for Akosua. To her parents, this was an effort to train her as a good housewife and prepare her for marriage. Neither of these ideas pleased Akosua because she was not happy and was scared by the thought of an arranged marriage.

Her half sisters and their friends had been paying more particular attention to their night studies, which they found to be very interesting. Night studies were very popular in the local high schools in Ghana. Supervision was a little bit loose. Akosua therefore asked permission from her parents to attend night studies. Each day from seven to ten o'clock in the evening, students would go to their schools for night studies and do their homework. However, the night studies were more than just homework. Various classes in the high schools used the time for brainstorming on problem topics, group discussions, and play.

There was one big electric lamp in Akosua's class. It was on top of a cupboard, which stood in the right corner of the classroom. Each student had smaller lamps on their desk. These were used as backup in case of power failure. During intermittent short breaks from night studies, the students gathered on the porch of the main school building and played cat and mouse games. Others just gossiped in an effort to release tension. They all studied and had fun during these hours. They were at several places on the school compound, gathered in groups. Usually, they gathered near the bathhouse or on the porch in front of the principal's office. The same old happiness always prevailed at night studies. Some students bought fried ripe plantain from the streets and ate in the corridors. Others who brought food from home gathered in other suitable places.

Akosua was not motivated to do any serious studing at home, but rather went to night studies each night. It was natural to meet with her friends at school because they were preparing for the examinations also. With her classmates around, she always had some good students available to help her in mathematics and other subjects. As the pending high school diploma examinations drew closer, she requested to do fewer household duties. A few days before the examination period her parents were less harsh on her.

She had all the necessary time to study and did what she wanted to do. Since there were no formal classes, they held private studies on common problems in Chemistry, Biology and Mathematics, in which some of the young women had problems. Akosua had other student partners to help her in Mathematics, Physics, and other science subjects during the night studies. Generally, the females were good in Geography, English, Art, or History, and they enjoyed Arts and Crafts, Cookery, Sewing, and other activities. This reinforced the old adage that the sciences were very hard and not meant for females; these were subjects for the men. However, this conventional idea was disputed in later years as more females graduated with honors in the sciences from many colleges.

One afternoon, Akosua was relaxing at home when Grace, her old girlfriend, called on her. Grace was the same age as Akosua, but lighter in complexion. She had some news. "Akosua, there is a new guy in town who does tutoring to get students ready for their diploma exams. This is a great chance for us, and I know the man personally. Let's do it," she suggested.

The man was called Williams, a professional guy on Fourth Street North in Akim Oda. After Grace mentioned this, Akosua readily followed because she knew Grace loved her and wanted her to pass the examination. They took a taxi straight to Mr. Williams' office.

"There he is." Grace pointed to Mr. Williams.

Mr. Williams was an older man in his fifties. He welcomed Akosua and Grace and briefed them on the various items on the program before registration. The tutorials available were only for the English examination. After a while, Grace followed him to the conference room. Akosua stayed behind. She was alone for about twenty minutes and started feeling sleepy and wanted to leave. When Mr. Williams returned, he asked Akosua some questions on her past English examinations. The two then listened while Mr. Williams showed them success stories of his program and testimonials from past students. Time was running fast for Akosua, so she signaled to Grace that they should be leaving. As they left the premises, Mr.

Williams whispered something to Akosua as if to make a pass at her. He gave them a sample English essay topic and guidelines to practice at home. Akosua and Grace thought the man was handsome, and both admired him. Neither of them complained nor made a comment about him.

At home, Akosua copied the essay format. They later agreed to pay him another visit after the examinations. Since it was three days before the examinations, Akosua had no choice but to inform her half sisters and other friends of the new English preparation guide. In fact, the man had given them a tip on the essay paper. He told them to prepare a paper on the happiest day in their lives. This topic as an English paper was very easy for Akosua. She did her research and sought assistance on the paper. She wrote it and had it corrected by other teachers who were good in English and essay writing. Soon the news had spread among all candidates in the school and other schools that there was a sure tip on the English paper. It was a simple matter of writing the story clearly with the appropriate English sentences.

An account of the happiest and most interesting day in one's life was not actually difficult. However, the examiners would be looking for sentence construction, spelling, use of phrases, vocabulary, and organization. To write about the happiest day in one's life could stir up one's most treasured memories and thoughts. The happiest day in Akosua's life could have been one of several. She could have considered the day when the Star Jokers came to town. That had been a very happy and memorable day for her. Essien gave her a treat, although he had wanted to force her to have sex. Akosua could remember another happy day in her life. It rained that day. It was a weekend and she had studies. She did not join the family on a trip to the farm. She was with Essien and they visited the local museum for the entire day. Essien had taken Akosua to lunch that day because it was her birthday. She could have prepared very well on all these scenes, and could have written perfectly on any of them. However, she felt they were not very interesting topics for the school examinations.

13

Finally, she chose a particular day when the old man was celebrating a family reunion festival at home. That day her mother gave her newly-designed family reunion clothes, and turkey soup was prepared. A sheep was slaughtered, and there was much to eat. Akim Oda Brass Band No. 2 provided music. The old man invited his friends. Grace came, too, since she was a close family friend. Mr. Mensah did the customary rites. After that, a local choir group sang two of their most popular tunes. The family reunion was full of fun. Everyone was happy and enjoyed that day. That was the reason Akousa chose this day for the topic of her essay. The family reunion celebrations were yearly events. However, that particular year was one of a kind. On this occasion, the research on Akosua's family history was made known, and a family tree was prepared on a large sheet of drawing paper. This was read out loud and distributed to all members. Special prayers were said for the departed ones. The family used the occasion to get to know each other. There were so many that it was very difficult to remember names. Akosua prepared this chosen topic very well. She placed emphasis on the importance of the family reunion which her father celebrated every year.

It was not surprising that Akosua was very nervous about the pending high school diploma examinations. It was the second Friday in June, a popular day for all schools. Grace called Akosua early that morning. With their pens, soft pencils, erasers, and rulers, they set off to their respective examination centers. There were more smart school boys and girls that morning than ever seen before. Essien called Akosua and wished her good luck. The big school bell rang five times, and they all entered the examination hall. The first paper was on geography. It was followed by math, biology, and a general paper, respectively. Since Akosua did not trust herself in the general paper, she was very careful. There was a five minute break between the papers, then came the English essay. Each candidate had very high expectations for this paper. Each had decided to write well, as planned.

The supervisor called the candidates to order, then held the large envelope containing the questions. He raised his voice and said, "I open these papers in the name of the Almighty." The supervisor then took the question papers out and distributed them face down on each desk. He then ordered, "Don't look or turn your papers over until you are told to do so." He repeated this twice. From the last row, he walked up to the front of the class and glanced at his watch. "Turn over, read, and start work," he shouted.

Akosua was still nervous. She tried to catch a glimpse of other candidates, hoping to see smiling faces. She was very hesitant to read the question paper. Finally when she read the paper, it was very different. Wow! The English essay was difficult. What a surprise! It was a clear shock. The essay was about "A Description of the Work of an Auditing Firm," showing problems faced by auditors in their profession.

"Could the examiners have been tricking us?" Akosua spoke to herself.

Other candidates had surprised looks on their faces. Yes, it was all over their faces! They could not blame their teachers, nor Mr. Williams with his so-called tutorial and preparation guides. The paper was just an unexpected one. None of the practice questions even came up. The candidates had no idea about auditing. The supervisor was strict. He took long strides through rows of desks and tables.

The candidates could not talk between themselves as they had wanted to. Sixty minutes passed away. Another thirty minutes passed. Akosua expected the supervisor to have stopped them by now. Without hesitation, he shouted, "Get ready to stop work."

A few minutes later he raised his voice and shouted, "Stop Work!"

The class was quiet. None of the preparation questions and examples had come up on the exams. Some students were happy about the whole examination, except for the English essay. Others, like Akosua, were more shocked and surprised. She suspected that some candidates thought the English essay examination was easy.

To those, the paper was not difficult. However, Akosua and others who had no ideas on auditing were shocked. Some of them found it hard to settle down to write anything meaningful. After the examinations were over, Akosua was worried about getting a passing grade on the English paper.

Later, some of her classmates called to sympathize with her on the English paper. Grace also called and suggested that they visit Mr. Williams to make a report. They agreed that Akosua would lunch with Essien first, and then meet Grace later. Akosua had planned not to go home immediately. She knew she would finish the examinations at midday that Friday, but she had informed her household that the examinations would be over at four o'clock in the afternoon. She could then use the four hours to celebrate in her own way. The fact that she had completed her high school education marked an important milestone in her life. It brought several thoughts to her about what she was going to do. All that advice from her mother about business and the expectations of an arranged marriage to an old, rich farmer were like dreams to her.

Her day was planned as she wanted, and she did her best to make good use of the time. She hurried to see Essien, hoping to meet Grace later. Essien was at home waiting in the backyard garden. Akosua never used the main entrance to visit Essien. She was always afraid that someone would report her to Mr. Mensah. Essien signaled her to pass through the rear gate entrance. He gave her soda and some biscuits. Essien could understand her feelings about the examinations and did not want to discuss anything on the English paper. After a a few minutes, he brought Akosua more food. It was light green soup and rice. After eating, Akosua requested to leave. She said good-bye to Essien, although Essien thought she would have stayed much longer. Her plan was to meet Grace and give a follow up report to Mr. Williams. Essien reluctantly understood her when she requested to leave.

Akosua took a short cut to her rendezvous with Grace. Grace was already waiting. She spoke quietly to Akosua. "You look smart and full of pleasures, dear," she said.

"Essien was simple and understanding," Akosua replied.

The two then turned toward the home of Mr. Williams at the northern end of town. They got there in a short time and found Mr. Williams. They were offered drinks, which they refused. Mr. Williams talked first, saying, "I heard your examinations were difficult."

"We are surprised. How the examiners could have presented such papers surprised everyone," Grace replied and continued, "Everyone has been complaining about the examination."

"I'm sure you are all worried," Mr. Williams continued.

"Ah, Mr. Williams, this may or may not be true. Some found it easy!" Akosua retorted.

After some discussions, Grace gave up because she was tired. Mr. Williams asked Akosua to wait in one of the living rooms. She felt a little bit uncomfortable. She was also very tired. Some minutes later, Akosua heard a struggle in the nearby living room. It was Grace and Mr. Williams. She heard a bang and a slap on a face. It was Grace attacking Mr. Williams.

Grace suddenly ran to Akosua. They left the premises very annoyed and worried. It was almost four o'clock in the evening, and they had to go home. Mr. Williams gave them twenty dollars to take a taxi as they left for home. They refused the offer. Akosua asked Grace about what had happened. She said the man had wanted to make love to her. "I slapped him during a struggle, so he ordered me off," Grace explained on their way.

Akosua got home as planned later in the day. Mr. Mensah's place was unusually quiet. She asked one of her half brothers about where everyone was. She learned that Mr. Mensah had taken his wives and the children off to a gospel church about three miles away to a religious service. Entering her room, she slept for a few hours before the household came home. The rest was good for Akosua because she was very tired. She knew it was going to take her some time before discussing her examinations with anyone in the house. That was, if anyone was interested at all. The thoughts of the day filled her. She thought of Essien and of the incident involving Grace and Mr. Williams. It was very hard to understand what had really happened. Maybe they should not have gone to Mr. Williams at all. She thought about home and her future, then fell asleep.

Later, the deafening noise of the children in the house woke her from sleep. The news was already circulating in the household that she had finished school. Mr. Mensah had gone upstairs. The old man was tired and had gone to bed. Mrs. Mensah entered Akosua's room. She stood by her bed and asked about the examinations. Akosua could not give any satisfactory reply. She got up from the bed because there was a special reason that had brought her mother to her room. She wanted Akosua to go to the kitchen and help prepare the soup for the day. Oh! Can you imagine? It was a turkey soup. A tiring dish to prepare for a meal.

After dinner, she was told that Mr. Mensah's friend, Papa James, the rich farmer, gave the turkey as a gift to her. It was to celebrate her completion of school. On hearing that, Akosua was so annoyed she wanted to vomit all the food out. She was also mad at her mother. After the meal, she washed the dishes, cleaned the kitchen, and threw the trash away. To keep herself busy, she scrubbed all the dirt off the kitchen walls. She decided not to worry about anyone. Her mother sat with her for a longer time than usual. As suspected, she wanted to talk Akosua into marriage; however Akosua brushed the subject aside any time it came up. Akosua went to bed very late that night with the hopes that no one in the household would ever bring up the subject of marriage again. As disturbed as she was, her intention was to keep herself busy and forget all the troubles at home, especially the trouble concerning the local rich farmer.

CHAPTER 2
Thoughts of the Future

September 1987

There was a rumor in Mr. Mensah's household and in the immediate neighborhood about the arranged marriage for Akosua. She had heard from her half-sister that the marriage proposal was all over the streets. This made Akosua very uncomfortable. She had also heard from some of her playmates, who laughed and teased her about this so-called marriage proposal. The possibility of an arranged marriage to this old local farmer who was already married scared Akosua. At almost eighteen and a half years, and just out of the local school, she was a young person with ambition. Her father had initiated and supported this old, aggressive male chauvinist in his riches seeking a new wife. Such an old man wanted to give a young lady like Akosua a sewing machine to stay at home and bear him children — a common thing in some of the old traditional African societies.

The following Sunday, she knew her mother would repeat her wishes to go to the missionary house that morning and follow up to the church to thank the Lord that she had completed her studies in the local high school. As usual, Akosua got up early and did her part of the jobs in the household. She took a bath and ironed her clothes. In reality, she also thought it was necessary that she go to church that morning. She wanted the blessing of the Lord to support her personal aspirations, but not the type being planned by her family with the old farmer.

Her dress was neat and beautiful; it was a white and blue cotton linen. The two left for the church service that morning. It was not a time to show herself to the public, so she walked as fast as she could to follow her mother. Akosua also expected Grace at the morning church service. They had talked about it briefly before.

Suddenly she heard a call, "Akosua!" She looked back and saw Essien. Time was not on her side because her mother was doubling her footsteps. She signaled to show him her mother's presence.

"Akosua," she heard the call again. The best and wisest thing she could do was pretend she heard no call. Her mother was an eavesdropper. She would report whatever she saw or heard about Akosua on the way to church to the old man and the people at home. Akosua hated insults. It was not pride! She was in no mood at that time for insults from Mr. Mensah.

They got to the church early. It was not surprising to see several of her mates and their relatives at the same mission. She saw their beautiful dresses. Julie was neatly dressed; so were Ruth and two other girls in the same pew. Akosua's dress was no comparison to theirs because some of these girls would do anything to dress in the most expensive outfits they could find. This would make them appear very neat, decent, and the talk of town. They would put on the most expensive clothing, even if it meant taking money from the older men they had been dating or matched with for a possible arranged marriage. Her dress was no comparison to theirs at all. The Reverend Minister was brief in his sermon. Mrs. Mensah offered twenty dollars as a tithing and Thanksgiving, while the parents of other mates gave over fifty dollars or more.

Grace was nowhere to be found. She did not come to church. Akosua asked her mother if she could visit Grace. She did not understand why Grace had not attended the church service. Akosua thought that maybe Grace was sick or that something must have prevented her from coming to the church. Mrs. Mensah did not indicate any sign of immediate approval. Akosua asked again. This time, Mrs. Mensah nodded in approval, but it seemed she wanted to go with her, or to make sure she returned home early. However, Akosua went in the direction to visit Grace, while her mother walked home.

"You should not be in town for long," Mrs. Mensah said. "Your father might need your services in the house," she continued.

The latter utterance made Akosua annoyed immediately because there were many boys and girls in the house. "My services are not special to anyone," Akosua said to herself.

As fast as she could walk, she left to see Grace. Back at home, later in the evening, she went straight to bed. In the days ahead, she was so mad at home that she had even forgotten to prepare for her prom party as she had discussed with Grace.

Although the final examinations were over, the prom party was not scheduled until several weeks after the examinations. The official school closing date was about a month away. Akosua informed Essien before the prom party that he was not going to be her date. She wanted no one. She no longer wanted Essien for her boy friend. She wanted no one in her way to disrupt her future. Essien was no longer on her mind. Although he was her high school sweetheart, Akosua thought it was a good idea to stop the relationship. At that stage in her life, she was in no mood for a male companion. Secondly, she wished to avoid any confrontation by her father, who had been entertaining the idea that Akosua marry the old farmer as soon as convenient.

The school compound was cleaned for the prom day. There were national and local flags all over the campus. Large banners welcomed parents who came to the party. Akosua could not prepare for the prom party at school as other girls because she refused to accept the new clothes given to her by Papa James. Her parents did not support her nor help her in the preparation of the prom party. Although she had been quarreling with them, they still gave her permission to attend the party as long as she was back home by eight in the evening. Akosua borrowed a nice dress from Grace and both attended the prom party at the school.

As could be expected, Akosua was very upset at the prom party because the teachers took the occasion to announce the various colleges that had offered admission to some of her classmates. Their names were mentioned. Accompanied by their parents and relatives, the admitted students received a standing ovation. Akosua felt very jealous. There was one girl who was accompanied by her future husband. Hers was also an arranged marriage. The so-called husband was old enough to be the girl's parent. Akosua did her best to ignore that couple, an elderly man who had found a new younger wife besides those he already had. It was polygamy at its worst.

She tried as best she could to make herself happy. They always had their funny little habits at school. This was part of them, and it made their lives full and meaningful. It was good. The sons and daughters of the rich brought many cakes and soft drinks. It was simple merry-making. But as seniors in the school, and it being leavers' day, they made sure that the organization of the party was to their interest. Grace kept her company always. They ate and ate as much food as they could at the party. The day was for them.

Grace left rather early. It was almost six in the evening. Akosua had to get home by eight. Although there was enough time for her to stay longer at the party, she left for home also. The household was indoors. She went upstairs to report to her father and thank him for allowing her out that night, then walked straight to her bedroom. She could tell from his face he was not happy.

The following Saturday morning, Akosua cleaned the compound and scrubbed the main bathroom in the house. It was the day when all the households had to follow Mr. Mensah to his farm. It was an interesting weekly routine. She would have enjoyed working on the farm that day, but thought otherwise. She had to see Grace. How and what excuse to give was her problem. After scrubbing the bathroom, she saw the boys in the house dressed to go to the farm. Suddenly, she heard, "Akosua! Akosua!" Her father called. He then also shouted for her half-sisters. "Mary! Kate! You should clean the backyard of the house and the compound," he ordered them. "You, Akosua, you should go to the local store later today to get groceries and prepare supper for me before I return," Mr. Mensah added. "Now, the rest, let's move!"

He shouted at the household and they marched and played with each other while Mr. Mensah trailed behind, slowly. Akosua watched them all go out of sight. The journey to the farm resembled an intentional parading of Mr. Mensah's children for people in Akim Oda to see his household. Traditionally, it was a sign of his manhood in the society that he had so many children. Fingers were pointed at him and comments made such as, "There goes Mr. Mensah's sons and daughters and grandchildren." This was what Mr. Mensah always wanted to hear. If this old man had such pride in showing off his household, Akosua saw no reason why he did not take any responsibility in furthering the education of his children in any higher institution.

"What was wrong with this man?" Akosua asked herself. Akosua compared Mr. Mensah to the head of the Brookman household. That man worked hard to send his children to good institutions. None of Mr. Mensah's eldest children was a lawyer, an engineer, a doctor, an architect, a teacher, or even a clerk. Most were unemployed or semi-employed. Steve always hung around the local cafeteria; John was a part-time bus stop cleaner, but most of the time unemployed. Titus was always at the Town Council, running errands for friends. Akosua could not continue mentioning their names. She never wanted to hear them again. After all, Mr. Mensah's household was not the only large one in the town. A look at the McKays, the Johnsons, the Basemans, Clements, and others, indicated they were all doing well in the town. To stay in this house under these hardships would be tantamount to a punishment for Akosua. These were the very thoughts that had been occupying her mind.

"With the rat out of sight, what else could the mice do but feel happy and be relieved of the tension in the house," she said to the rest of the household.

Joined by her half-sisters, Akosua cleaned, scrubbed, and tidied the big house. Time went very fast, and soon it was twelve o'clock. The household would return by six o'clock in the evening. Akosua still had some time to go the store via Grace. She got there in no time. Lucky young woman, Grace was still in her morning gown. When Akosua disclosed her itinerary to her, they planned to be at Grace's home for a while and later do the grocery shopping together. For the two hours she was with Grace, all the thoughts and problems at home faded as if they never existed. It seemed her whole world now was with Grace.

They talked a lot about themselves. Grace made Akosua aware that she had been facing similar problems in her household. She had been advised by her parents to marry a man in the town. Akosua did not bother much to find out who the man was. The very thought of that idea made her sympathize with Grace. It brought their relationship much closer and made it stronger.

Grace mentioned her Aunt Rose, who was coming home from Lagos in Nigeria. Grace planned to join her on the return journey to seek greener pastures and leave Ghana for good. Akosua listened very carefully with much interest and wished her the best of luck. She also expressed her interest to join them whenever that opportunity arose, if Grace would only mention it to her Aunt when she arrived. The two later stopped their conversation and went to get groceries.

Akosua got home early and prepared dinner for her father. About five-thirty, she saw the first boy from the farm carrying a very big load of firewood on his head, followed by others. "Yes, there they come," she said to herself, "the Mr. Mensah delegation."

The boys carrying firewood raced toward home. They ran

after each other to see who would arrive home first. The younger children and the girls followed but did not run or compete. The women followed with their babies while Mr. Mensah stayed very late at the farm with his most loving wife for that particular day. He eventually came home for his dinner. Since Mr. Mensah knew that Akosua would not waste time with his dinner, he walked upstairs into his room and called her for the grocery receipt and the balance of the money used. Not surprising, he did not ask Akosua about the examination, let alone ask about her educational goals and aspirations for the future. She knew her father would never ask. It was not important to him. He would have wished that the old farmer man had come around much earlier and proposed marriage. That was the reason the two of them had been spending much time together.

"Does he think he could get a dowry through me?" Akosua asked herself. "Never in my life! I am a young woman of initiative and charisma, and the future depends on me. I could never support a man in an arranged marriage. In such a domestic life, I would be grounded as a subservient wife for the rest of my life."

With full knowledge about these developments, Akosua knew it was time for her to leave the household. She was determined to avoid this marriage. She had seen other young women graduating from schools and colleges with degrees and becoming career women, with just a little support from their parents. At this time, she had her future educational plans as her top priority, not the marriage idea being pushed by her parents. She had been discussing this with Grace.

Everything looked so uncertain to her. She knew if she stayed in the town, she would be forced into marriage and given away to the old man against her wishes. This seemed very strange to her, but it was the old social and cultural way of life. However, it was gradually changing for the better. Due to educational opportunities, some young women had come out of the bondage of old cultural beliefs. Many were working as career professionals in the cities. She wanted to be like them. However, Mr. Mensah refused to understand these changes in the society. He was not interested in Akosua's future educational plans. With desperation and anger, Akosua could not control her temper at times. She realized then that she had to leave Ghana.

"But through whom, and by which route to where, or to do what?" she asked herself. If any opportunity had come her way, she would have left the home of Mr. Mensah immediately after her high school examinations. She knew, however, that this required careful planning. Akim Oda was her birth place. Born in the post-independence young generation baby boom, she wanted to work hard and plan her own life. All that was required was a higher education. It was an adventure to see the world. After a possible education and a career, she could then find someone whom she would love. Thoughts on these issues engaged her mind every day, not the turkey and gifts from the old farmer. Akosua's mind had no place for that. She was serious about furthering her education.

Akosua went to bed at the end of the day and slept deeply that night. Before she went to sleep, she thought again of Ghana, the society, groups, clans, individuals, and about the tribes competing for limited resources. She thought of how she had chosen to complete high school. Her future seemed so uncertain. Would she be enrolled in a college or vocational trade school? Akosua could not predict her future. She had no answers to her own questions.

Waking up the following morning, Akosua found that all her thoughts were really past dreams she had once had. The society at home was not very different from any other African town after the years when the white man left. It was not that her ambition was very high. The truth was that under prevailing conditions, opportunities, and social constraints, education was much more important. It was also much more important for the illiterate and half-educated women working forty to fifty hours a week to support their families while some of their lazy men drank beer all day. Traditionally in the villages, the majority of the women with little or no education did much of the work to support the household and raise families. With very little or no respect from society, it was difficult for many women to choose professional careers and improve the quality of life for themselves and others. Some change was in progress, but it was very slow.

The change was easier for families with a higher education. It was easier if the head of the household was literate and understood the importance of education. Higher education was the catalyst that propelled the change. Other families guided and supported their daughters in the schools and colleges in the country. Akosua felt jealous of some friends in the town. There were several opportunities for the youth in Ghana; there were reputable community colleges in the urban centers that offered various special courses for those who could not make it easily to the universities and professional schools. There were also the Teacher Training Colleges designed for high school graduates. No matter which way you viewed it, education was a priority program. However, the effort depended on your family and the individual.

There was the premier university in the capital town, there was the great technical university and the educational center on the coast, not to mention the numerous historic missionary schools and colleges, most dating back to the early nineteenth century. To make education meaningful, the government built many high schools. One was located in each local government area. These were the government educational trust schools and colleges. Akosua could foresee a nation at least on a path to development. Education was compulsory at the primary level. Students in various colleges and secondary schools usually inspired the youth in high schools.

When colleges reopened or closed, one could see the college students in chartered buses singing. It was very easy to tell which particular school or college the group belonged by the abbreviated inscriptions on the buses. These inscriptions were abbreviations of the college names. Akosua could remember the notations for the very popular schools. Thus, on a bus chartered by students of St. Augustine's College, the inscription read "AUGUSCO." The Adisadel College was "ADISCO." For Solomon College, it was "SOLOCO." "ABUSCO" stood for Abuakwa State College, and so on.

Akosua wished to be among them. She could imagine the enthusiasm and the pride of these students. She wished she had enough parental support to give her an atmosphere conducive to writing the College Examination. That was why she had struggled to get through four years of high school to complete her high school education. It was possible under the educational system in Ghana to enter college from high school, as long as you passed the college entrance examinations. Akosua could have entered college had she written the College Entrance Examination earlier on. It was not her fault.

"Oh, Akosua," she said to herself, "there could have been a way out!" The truth was that when she started high school, she approached her father to give her money to register for the College Entrance Examination. Mr. Mensah refused and referred Akosua to her mother. Her mother did not have the money. Mr. Mensah did not understand Akosua. It was not his fault, she thought. Mr. Mensah had not had much education himself. As such, Akosua could not register for the examination. Mr. Mensah understood nothing about what the government was doing to make education meaningful for all its citizens.

When she had approached Mr. Mensah to ask about the College Entrance Examinations, Mr. Mensah shouted at her saying, "You up and coming girls are attracted by all this useless propaganda. You want to go to college! Akosua! Would you be going to school all your life and get married to your books?"

It was too much for Akosua. The old man just wanted her to get married, even at the earlier age. He saw nothing good in education. He believed a girl did not need all that education. There was nothing she could have done then. She was under his care. Akosua had to continue high school. She never understood her father. She took consolation, however, because out of his many children, she could not identify even one whom he had sponsored for college education. There was only Patrick; however, he had left and forgotten about the old man. He was enrolled at the Academy College with much financial and moral support from an uncle and some other relatives. Mr. Mensah did not care that much about him.

Patrick was an older son, much older than Akosua. She had written several letters to Patrick at his school informing him of her plight. He replied to Akosua as a true brother, saying that if she wanted to continue her education, she should not look up to her father, but rather talk to other relatives, or at least look for a loan to support herself initially.

After discussions with her mother, Akosua noticed that she was less interested, just as the old man. Her mother was also thinking about how Akosua could get married to this old man in the village and settle to raise children so that she could have more grandchildren to play with. Akosua never realized how painful and insulting their suggestions were until she pondered over them. After several discussions with other distant relatives, there was no help coming from any place. She made a bold decision that was not the news her parents wanted to hear. She told them she had decided she was not going to be a party to any arranged marriage proposals initiated by any relative. She would have been happy to have her future educational plans discussed.

Akosua thought the choice of marriage partner was a personal but mutual decision between parents and their sons and daughters. It should never be imposed or forced. The world was still wide open for her, and society was going through major technological, social, and economic transformations. The old order that refused any changes was being left behind. She did not want to be a part of the latter. Her mind was made up. It seemed to her that Mr. Mensah's family did not really need her.

Akosua was young, gifted, and beautiful. She was a girl with ambition. Even if it was not possible for her parents to help her make an academic life, her desire and willpower were very strong. She would find other sources of finance for her college tuition in the future, even if that meant by any legal means necessary. The thought about competition in this world was high on her mind but very much open. After years of formal elementary and high school education, she could not just go waste in someone's household. She had come of age and could see the changing society better than her old folks at home.

Akosua thought about her future. Her thoughts were filled with worries, and her eyes with tears for the next fortnight. Her household duties from then on were done with little enthusiasm. She became unhappy and a recluse in her own household. She knew that a change must come to her life. There was a need to hurry because her anger and impatience were growing day by day, and it was getting worse. She stayed at home for over four more weeks. She thought of Grace. All this time, she had not had the opportunity to discuss in detail what was happening to Grace and her similar problem at her home.

Akosua thought of visiting Grace, the only one with whom she could discuss her future. She remembered Grace had mentioned a proposed trip. It was a journey to join Aunt Rose in Nigeria. It was the only way to escape the wrath of her home. She knew it was suicidal to run away from home, especially being a young girl. There was nothing she could have done, however. At any opportunity, she was prepared to leave the household for good.

There were several factors to push her out of Ghana. The country had witnessed rapid development in the fifties under the white man's rule, until it attained its independence in 1957. Primary education was made compulsory immediately after the independence era, and infrastructure was improved. There was a rise in the manufacturing sector, which depended on imported raw materials. There was a decline in agriculture and a fall in the price of its mono crop, cocoa. Ghana, according to its first black leader, a great Pan-African, was the home of every African. Africans from Nigeria, and all the way from South Africa, came to live in Ghana. All Africans, even other than the citizens of Ghana, had enjoyed scholarship grants to higher education. As economic growth slowed and the world political arena became complex in a changing social and economic setting, the outward migration from Ghana began. Nigeria and Ghana were the noted countries in the West African region due to pace of development, common foreign language, and identical environs.

Akosua's own problems at home certainly were immediate causes that awakened her desire to leave Ghana. Her future education goals had been paralyzed. Her future was bleak and very uncertain. She had no career training and there was no possibility that her parents would encourage her to attend a higher college. She hated marriage at that time, and certainly did not want to be forced into it. Her mind was made up.

She had planned to make use of the least opportunity that came her way. She imagined the consequences of her planned actions. She was prepared for anything. The more she saw her other mates having their educations and futures planned with the help of their parents, the more she felt jealous and the greater her desire to move out despite any consequences. She believed for a parent to refuse educational opportunities to a child was very regrettable. This could have only happened in such an uneducated and polygamous home. She did not want to be a part of a home with such an absence of intellectual structure.

CHAPTER 3
Journey of Hope

December, 1987

Grace invited Akosua to her house in the latter part of the week. Grace apologized for staying away from Akosua for some time. Upon arrival, Akosua noticed Grace was packing her clothing. "Grace, what is happening?" Akosua asked.

Grace replied, "Akosua, it is very unfortunate, but the relationship with my family is now very serious. I could not inform you of what has happened in the past few weeks. My family has also arranged a marriage for me without my consent. They want me to join the man — an old, rich, traditional man, as soon as possible. I have been unable to inform you of these latest pressures from my household. I am fed up in this house!"

"What are you saying, Grace?" Akosua asked.

"I have plans to travel with my Aunt Rose to Nigeria. My family does not know about this arrangement. As I had earlier mentioned to you, she came some weeks ago and is leaving soon. She lives in Lagos. We would travel by road."

This was a surprise to Akosua. She realized that Grace's problem was more immediate and very serious. Akosua said to herself, "Education! Education! Going to school with difficulties. Oppression in the household, and a disrespect for the young, modern woman. An arranged marriage! It could not be in my generation!"

"Grace, I would like to join you," Akosua requested. "I will not let this old Mr. Mensah make me a fool in this modern society. Would you mind?" Akosua asked.

"Oh, no! We can travel together. I have already informed my aunt of your troubles; she said you can come along provided you are prepared," Grace replied.

Back at home, Akosua went straight to her mother and informed her that she wanted to leave the next morning to visit their cousin Mrs. Fati who lived about ten miles way. Her mother hesitated but later agreed after consulting Mr. Mensah. Mrs. Fati was a direct cousin who lived in Awisa, a different town. She was always sending invitations to Akosua for a visit. Akosua's mother suggested that Akosua return by sunset the day after. Akosua packed her clothing that night. She did not take many items to avoid any suspicion at home. The following morning, Akosua said good-bye to her mother and promised to be back by evening the day after. Instead, she went straight to Grace's house.

Grace introduced Akosua to her Aunt Rose and they were on their way to Lagos in no time. Aunt Rose had been in Nigeria for several years doing business, though they never knew what it was. Grace informed Akosua of this before they left; however, they guessed her business. She was very rich and was in contact with Lagos socialites. Akosua had a very good impression of her. She was quite good looking, hardworking, forceful, and very liberal-minded. Akosua learned from Grace before their departure that Aunt Rose had been to school at the popular Akim Oda Girls Boarding School in Ghana. After school, she worked for a year and then entered a technical institute. With a Diploma in Catering and Hotel Management, she went to Lagos when conditions started to retrogress at home due to slow economic growth. She settled in Ikeja in Lagos.

The three went to the transport station and boarded a bus. After a three-hour journey, Akosua thought they would relax for a while when they came to a rest stop, but to her astonishment they immediately boarded another bus heading for Lagos. There was heavy traffic on the highway between Ghana and Nigeria. The traffic included both traders and migrants. The reasons for the intensive activities could be traced to the economy of Ghana and other surrounding countries at that time. It was not very strong compared to the oil boom in Nigeria. At home, due to the massive education programs and the slow growth of the economy, graduates from the institutions had not found professional jobs. The economy had not been able to absorb the high number of graduates in the country. As such, one saw numbers of unemployed and semi-skilled graduates daily on the streets. This also resulted in a very high labor migration to other neighboring countries with somewhat stable or higher-growth economies. The labor migration was so serious that at times it was impossible to find a member of a graduating class from the universities still living in Ghana. The economic situation was a deterrent to a good living for some of the graduates.

Akosua could not stand the problems at home, either. She guessed that the lack of job openings could have been one of the reasons why her father was not even interested in her future education. Mr. Mensah had wanted to give her for marriage. She left and did not regret it. She was eighteen and a half years old, black and beautiful. She followed her friend to Lagos, the sprawling oil rich city, for an adventure.

On their way, the bus developed a problem at Coutonou, a French-speaking city along the coast. A mechanic on the bus attended to it for over an hour. On the bus were a number of passengers, both black and white. A guy named Paul, a Peace Corps member from the United States, was on the bus. Paul had just completed his Peace Corps contract in Ghana and had taken on a volunteer job by himself in Nigeria for adventure. Coincidentally, Paul had been assigned at Akim Oda in Ghana during part of his Peace Corps contract. He was on his way to his new post in Nigeria.

Akosua talked to Paul for a while. He gave her his address,

so she could call on him later in Nigeria. It was already seven o'clock in the evening. Grace, her Aunt, and Akosua decided to sleep on the bus as other passengers had planned. Grace talked to the mechanic who said it was okay to sleep on the bus while it was being repaired. They could not find the driver. Later, upon inquiries, they learned he had gone to town to find some food to eat, leaving his co-driver behind.

Thoughts filled Akosua's mind. That was the idea of living. Man must eat! This driver could have gone with his co-driver or even ordered food so that both could have eaten together. But there sat the co-driver looking as hungry as ever. Grace's Aunt immediately brought out a very big Thermos and a food container. Yes, this woman was prepared. She dished out rice and gravy. Akosua ate with Grace. It was delicious. Aunt Rose also dished out a plate for the co-driver. She invited Paul to join them for the meal. Paul thanked them, but politely refused.

Within a blink of an eye, the co-driver had finished everything and was licking his plate clean. Men on the road hardly got the time to find good food to eat. Paul and other passengers on the bus could not help laughing.

It was almost midnight when they heard a whistle from a traffic police officer. He stood very close to the bus and asked the co-driver some questions. The passengers realized that the driver had parked the bus improperly. The policeman then came closer to the passengers and started checking their identity cards. He spoke to the co-driver in French, which Akosua did not understand. Surprisingly, Aunt Rose translated the language to English. Back home in Ghana, because the region was surrounded by French-speaking nations, French was taught in schools, but it was only in theory. The students never spoke it orally except sometimes in class. It was a poor application of a good educational policy in Ghana.

The policeman then asked all passengers to go to a rest area close to the beach to sleep. They could join the bus the following morning while it was been repaired. This was a good idea. Grace, Aunt Rose, and Akosua looked at each other. They and the other passengers on the bus left, walking slowly with their hand luggage, behind each other. The rest area was not far. On arrival, they found there were several other stranded travelers in a spacious hall. Men, women, and children were all jammed together. There were about thirty people, including the passengers from the bus. This idea of providing sleeping beds at a police rest area for stranded travelers was noble. Although conditions were not very comfortable, at least a form of satisfaction was guaranteed.

Paul did not sleep but read a book as they waited. There were many police officers in the room. One of them approached Aunt Rose and suggested the women sleep in a separate room next to the main hall. Immediately, Akosua felt a little bit suspicious. She thought of it as an opportunity for the policemen to make passes at the women. She had heard and read about past incidents some years ago. It had been done to other travelers previously. However, with Grace and her Aunt, Akosua felt confident that nothing of that sort would happen.

As they slept and relaxed, Akosua felt like using the bathroom. She got up and was walking through the corridor toward the bathroom, when a tall policeman in civilian clothes, but still displaying a badge, approached her as if he also wanted to use the bathroom. Akosua immediately turned back, but the police officer held her. He took her to another room and made an effort to force her to have sex. Akosua screamed; from nowhere came Paul. He was not asleep and had heard all the noise in the corridor. Seeing the white guy, the policeman ran as fast as he could. Akosua thanked Paul and went to their room. She immediately woke Aunt Rose and Grace. Akosua told them what had happened. They all got up and walked to the police duty officer to report the matter to him. Paul was already there and had told the duty officer what he had seen. The duty officer claimed it could not have been a policeman from the station, but rather someone from the town. They went back to their rooms, but could not sleep.

Akosua started thinking about her parents at Akim Oda. The adventure she had been praying for was now actually being experienced. She told herself that she must gather courage to face the unexpected.

At sunrise, Akosua, Grace and Paul walked to the beach to enjoy the scenery. Others were still at the police rest stop. Aunt Rose also stayed behind talking to the policemen about the incident the previous night. The beautiful lights in the morning in this French-speaking territory impressed Akosua. From the police rest stop she could view the Atlantic Ocean. The sun was coming out from afar. The sea breeze was excellent. She saw all the beautiful hotels along the coast. There were mostly white tourists from France on the beach. Some were playing tennis; others were setting up their beach umbrellas ready to sunbathe. The beautiful scenery made her think twice. She could see the government offices far away. Their location next to the hotels was to increase accessibility to the white business people and tourists at the hotels. It was not surprising to Akosua that there was hardly a black person around. These hotels were so expensive that they were above the income of the local people.

Aunt Rose called for their attention later, telling them that the bus was ready. It had been repaired and was ready to take off that afternoon. Grace and Akosua walked back, leaving Paul behind. They took a hot shower in the public rest area. Aunt Rose was already dressed. She looked very polished and was speaking to one police officer in English. Akosua eavesdropped and noticed the officer had given Aunt Rose names of some people to contact on their route, in case there were problems with other police officers. In this part of the world, traffic policemen took advantage of the high illiteracy rate and poverty among a large section of the society. For the most part, they did anything they pleased. They took bribes and delayed motorists as they wanted. They went unpunished because corruption ran throughout the hierarchy. Aunt Rose was getting names so they could have a safe and smooth journey.

Back on the bus, they were almost ready to go when another police officer came close to the bus. The driver told him the problem he had with the bus, then started a long conversation about other mechanical problems and how he had always struggled to repair. The officer gave the driver an address of a friend in Lagos at the border post whom he was to contact on the journey. The bus sped off at seventy miles per hour. The vegetation all along the coast on the way to Lagos was interchanging. In some areas there were coastal savannas; in other areas there were coconut plantations, semi-forests, and other varieties. Akosua did not see any major settlements, except dispersed mud huts belonging to the many people fishing on the coast.

One other noticeable feature was the use of mopeds, scooters, bicycles, and tricycles, sharing the same road with motor vehicles, heavy trucks, and buses. The mopeds were very much in use in these French-speaking West African countries. The car ownership ratios were very low; therefore, the use of mopeds was normal, on these roads. This was strange to Akosua. She began to realize that African countries were very diverse in many things. She had a lot to learn as they continued the journey.

The driver stopped again upon hearing the siren of a traffic police. After a brief conversation, the driver continued the journey. The passengers assumed he was acquainted with the police on the roads. He later parked the bus by the roadside again, and the passengers prayed he could put the bus back on the road. It would have been awful for them to be stranded again, let alone on the highway under the scorching sun. About five minutes later, the journey continued. Within an hour they were at the border.

The passengers exclaimed with joy that the journey was coming to an end. At last they could finally see Lagos in the distance. Grace and Aunt Rose tried to catch glimpses of Akosua's reactions. Their eyes sometimes met. They noticed Akosua was not disturbed. She looked upbeat, very normal. Aunt Rose had had several experiences at this border some years ago. She was used to the hustle and bustle, the daily activities, and the people.

Akosua imagined this was going to be the beginning of her new life in the great city of Lagos. Neither Aunt Rose, Grace, nor Akosua talked about anything they saw. There were so many things going on at the border that one had to keep a close watch on one's luggage. Like a parent, Aunt Rose paid for everything on their way. Paul waved good-bye to Akosua and then checked through the border. Aunt Rose and her party, however, entered a nearby restaurant. Looking through the window, they saw other people being led to a detour around the border. They were not using the formal border checkpoint. It was only then that Aunt Rose asked Grace and Akosua about their travel documents. They had none. Aunt Rose had not asked before they left Ghana because she thought Grace and Akosua were adults and that they would have known. She kept quiet for a while, then blamed herself for not preparing the travel documents for Grace and Akosua prior to leaving Ghana. They had no choice then but to find a way to avoid the checkpoint.

As they sat, they saw about fifty people far away trying to cross the border simultaneously. With confidence they sat at the restaurant and had some meat and soft drinks. Soon after the meal, a man in his thirties entered and talked to Aunt Rose. Akosua saw her give an envelope to the man. The man went out and returned about five minutes later with some other men. They took their luggage and Aunt Rose saw them off.

"Akosua," Aunt Rose called.

"Yes, Aunt," she answered.

"Grace," she called again.

"Yes, Aunt," Grace also answered.

Grace and Akosua knew they had to follow the call. Confidently they followed Aunt Rose down a long corridor and waited to cross the border. They went out to an open area to relax. They were surprised that Aunt Rose seemed to know almost all the people selling groceries. This was more of an informal open air market just before the border crossing. Her public relations and social interaction had been excellent and were a part of her. It was also very easy for her to make friends anytime in new environments.

Akosua knew the reason, then, why Aunt Rose had been having her way around easily. She was bold and adventurous. However, she had had a few set backs and problems in her life, as she did not practice the profession she learned at college. Akosua wondered whether this upset Aunt Rose at times.

While waiting, someone brought their entry passes to them. Aunt Rose gave something to the gentleman, and they all left to cross the border. They did not join or wait in the long line. It saved time, as they did not go through all the customs procedures and searches. Akosua thought the people doing this might be enriching themselves at the expense of the government. One could not count the number of people crossing. It was in the hundreds. Akosua noticed that the border posts were merely rubber stamps: an artificial border, indeed. She noticed some passengers alighted from buses and did not use the established checkpoints. They paid money depending on their goods and the possession of valid travel documents. They had to pay more if they possessed no valid documents.

Akosua recollected that there were about four different detour paths one could use to cross the border. One just had to pay at each spot. It was nothing but bribery. She noticed, also, that there were guides who collected a fee and took people through a bush path, a much more dangerous route to Lagos. A third option, a somewhat unofficial, border crossing was to board special vehicles heading directly to Lagos. Under this system, one paid a higher amount to the driver in charge of the particular bus. All passengers would then cross the border unchecked. The drivers sometimes collected your travel documents. This was usually an arrangement between drivers and the immigration and custom officials. On the average, Akosua noticed about a hundred people at a time moving into Lagos from all directions.

This border was notorious for illegal activities. One could not even count the number of hawkers and other retail salespersons all over the area. You could buy any form of currency in the world at the border. The American dollar reigned; however, some of the bills looked so dirty that Akosua did not want to touch them. They had passed from hand to hand, from underwear and pantyhose, and from pockets to a thousand and one pockets. This was the black market currency at the border.

Aunt Rose had briefed them about the scene at this border several times. Akosua had also learned a lot before from her schoolmates. She had also read the newspapers. The bribery at the border was just part of the larger corruption that sprang up during the oil boom in Nigeria. The country had suddenly been transformed into an oil rich economy. This was a country where the oil wealth was seen as booty to be looted by few individuals who cared less about the national economy. Due to the fact that the oil wealth was poorly distributed, almost everyone who had no access to the booty engaged in bribery to enrich himself. It was not one's fault if he or she had to find a new path to the riches in Lagos.

"It would therefore not be my fault, as I was supposed to search for a new life and a way to finance my future education. This is the place for me," Akosua murmured to herself.

Aunt Rose carefully described the links and economic activities that went on daily at the border between the adjacent countries. Akosua learned that first there had been an historical link between the people in the area. The border separated the people of Nigeria from other blacks in the neighboring countries. She learned that historically the people on either side of the border were of the same clan lineage, but it was the pattern of colonization and wars that separated them — a separation demanded by the greed of the

At the border in Lagos, Nigeria
Aunt Rose, Grace & Akosua

colonizers. While watching all these activities, thoughts of border separations of people of similar cultures were high on her mind. Each black person she saw resembled the other. Languages and forms of music were very similar. However, the people were of different nationalities. She could not imagine a society divided by an artificial boundary such as these country borders. These were basically the same people with a common culture — a related culture though different in practice, but based on similar traditional beliefs and objectives. They were all black, brought up on the coastal lagoon fringes and the tropical forests. They were recognized by the primary occupation of fishing and hunting. Akosua had also learned many lessons on history from her school in Ghana. She tried to relate what she learned in school to what she saw and heard at the border. This was an area demarcated by a political boundary into distinct countries. This was improper. Akosua kept wondering. She thought the colonial governments that had scrambled for the land, had in some ways done more harm than good to the people.

Aunt Rose led them outside the corridors of the immigration post. They were given special attention until they left. At last they were on the Lagos side of the border. On this side Akosua was surprised to see the number of restaurants. International and popular local dishes were served. Fufu, traditional food of the West African coast, was served everywhere. In Ghana it was prepared with yam or cocoyam or plantain. The soft food was made into a ball and eaten with a bowl of soup.

Aunt Rose, Grace, and Akosua passed by one of the Fufu restaurants. Aunt Rose gave a message to the owner of the restaurant. Akosua could not describe the scene she saw. There were many citizens of Ghana here. Some were eating, others drinking.

"Hum," she said to herself, "most of these boys and girls look tired either from the time spent on their journey or from the work they have been doing."

"Akosua," Aunt Rose called, "you may have a seat." Grace

had already sat down. Aunt Rose, as usual, went on chatting with the woman selling the food. One woman was speaking the local Ghana language. No doubt these languages were also noted on routes along the coast. There were people from Ghana and from almost all the English and French countries along the coast from West to East at this side of the border. Akosua's estimate of boys and girls from Ghana at the border was over twenty. It was not difficult to ascertain the level of education of these boys and girls from their conversation. No doubt they were products of the secondary education system. Unfortunately for them, they could not further their education. Opportunities for higher education had been very limited.

The competition was so tough for an education that you had to have both the brains and the finances to continue in any higher institution. Unfortunate ones, like Akosua and other dropouts, were thrust into society educated, even if it meant only being able to read and write at the high school level, yet they were unable to obtain a profession. Thus, there were many youths, economically active but without skills, vocations, or professions. Adventurous ones would travel to seek opportunities elsewhere, rather than stay under the declining economies of Ghana, where even the learned ones were moving out due to lack of jobs. An exodus indeed!

Within a matter of minutes, they were packing into a taxi heading toward downtown Lagos. It was not surprising that Aunt Rose was acknowledged here and there. After talking to a tall immigration officer, the taxi took off. Akosua noticed how briskly the transportation business was carried on in Lagos. Passengers and bus conductors were equally smart. The road from the border to Lagos was a first-class freeway. Akosua realized how the oil wealth had efficiently transformed the country and improved transportation. The freeways were the tunnels and spines of the total landscape. The stretch of landscape between the border and the city was vast.

Akosua had learned much about Lagos from school. She remembered a lot about the big city. She knew it used to be an old commercial center and a slave-trading town. In the seventeenth century, some of the locals were captured by force and taken to the Americas to work. Lagos was one of the major ports from where ships transported black people to the Americas. These were unfortunate historical times. She thought about slavery. The black people in the world had undergone much pain in those years. There had been several theories on slavery. It had hurt the people from the African continent. On ethical grounds, slave labor was an insult to the human race. The philosophy and pride of the African personality had been dented and tainted. As they continued on their way to Lagos, her thoughts on these stories became widespread.

It was the first time Akosua had set foot on the soil of another large English-speaking country in Africa. She had seen a lot of people from Lagos living in Ghana. On the other hand, Akosua felt a form of guilt within her when she set foot on the Lagos soil. Her guilt was due to the fact that Ghana's leader, a sociologist by profession, had enacted the Alien Compliance Order of the 1970s. It affected a lot of foreign nationals, especially the people from Lagos, residing in Ghana. As a sociologist, the leader should have thought twice on the repercussions of the policy. The Alien Compliance Order deported mainly the people of Nigeria from Ghana. It was a very bad policy. Until the partitioning of the dark continent, the people were basically in one territory, separated only by ethnic groupings. Dialects of languages were similar in several aspects; cultural traditions among the Africans were identical. The partitioning created political divisions. The sense of belonging, of being one, diminished. A larger percentage of migrants, it was noted, knew little of residence permits and regulations of stay.

Akosua's thoughts centered on the fact that such ignorance prompted the enactment of the Alien Compliance Order in Ghana. At one time, it might have been necessary in the country, upon assessment of its economic interests, and local support enforced compliance with the law. However, the manner in which it was carried out and the historical linkages between the countries of Nigeria and Ghana made the policy very inappropriate and very bad. The repercussions of that policy were evident in the mockery being made of the thousands of people migrating by any means necessary from Ghana to Nigeria. In the 1980's. Ghana was then in a very serious economic decline.

"What will happen to me if the authorities in Nigeria enact a similar policy and drive all of us out back to Ghana," Akosua asked herself. She thought about this and foresaw that it might happen one day. She prayed, however, that it would not happen during her temporal stay in Lagos. She felt very sad about this policy; she felt very guilty.

They got off at a bus stop in Lagos. Akosua noticed nothing was standing still. She could not compare the activities in this city to any city in Ghana. Lagos was a fast-paced, beautiful, big city. Ghana was very quiet by comparison. Lagos, she understood, had about six million people in its metropolitan area. The city itself had about one and a half million. Yes, it was her first time in a very big city. At least she knew the federal capital, though it would be moved after a new capital had been completed. She also knew that the population of Nigeria was large, about a hundred million or more. However, it had been impossible to conduct a decent census for the past decades in the country because of competing data on population densities between ethnic groups. Each attempt at a census resulted in tribal conflicts. The allocation of federal funds depended on the population distribution. The population was made up of three major ethnic groups, each believed to outnumber the other. There were many other groups she did not know about.

Akosua did not have much problem with adjustment. She wondered at first if the language would be difficult to learn; however, some accents were similar to that of Ghana. Activities were at a brisk pace. Open markets and traders occupied almost every available space. One could only count human heads. Grace gave her

Aunt a helping hand in carrying the luggage. Akosua helped with other luggage. They quickly followed a crowd crossing a busy intersection. Aunt Rose made them aware that the buses did not stop for passengers in Lagos. You board and jump out as they tailgate or idle closer to a stop sign. Just as they reached the bus stop, one came in and they ran as fast as they could with their luggage and boarded the bus. They all gasped for breath on the bus. It was crowded. The bus built to carry forty passengers had almost twice the number. It was a miracle how they even got on the bus. As the bus moved, a conductor squeezed himself between passengers collecting the bus fare. It was noisy on the bus with music at its highest volume. Akosua became a little agitated. The bus drove along a busy four-lane freeway. These roads had been built during the oil boom. The roads were wide and had pedestrian bridges all over them.

Akousa noticed two interesting items at the intersections, no motorist obeyed the yield sign and the overhead pedestrian bridges were not being used. The pedestrian bridges in the city were built to control the huge number of pedestrians who try to cross to the freeway. Instead, they stood by the freeway and looked in the direction of incoming vehicles traveling over sixty miles an hour. They would cross to the island if a small gap of time was available before the next vehicle passed by. The same was done with the vehicles coming from the opposite direction. The bus was now travelling further away from the city and later stopped a place called Anthony Station.

Akosua looked like a newcomer in a city. Everything was strange to her. Everything was new and everything moved swiftly around her. There was no time to ask questions or delay. Aunt Rose warned them to walk smart and pay attention to no one, but to follow her steps and keep a close eye on their luggage, or they could be stolen in a second. At Anthony Station, they immediately boarded another bus. Akosua sat in the front of the vehicle with Aunt Rose. She greeted the driver in English and a conversation started between the two as if they knew each other previously. After a short while on the bus, Akosua noticed they were getting further and further out of town. Development was not as intense; they had approached the fringes of Lagos.

They exited the bus at an unorganized bus stop, crossed the road, and entered a settlement, more or less a cluster village, called Cresthill in Ikeja, at the northeastern area on the outskirts of Lagos. Aunt Rose led; Grace and Akosua followed. As they walked through the village, Akosua noticed that Aunt Rose was popular here, too. Everyone they met greeted Aunt Rose. Akosua looked bewildered. Children, men, and women welcomed them. Akosua wondered what could have made Aunt Rose so popular in the area. From Grace, Akosua learned Aunt Rose had been living in the village for two years. Since it was a small area, community patterns were known and faces were very familiar to others in the community.

They entered an L-shaped block. It looked uncompleted. It was, however, in good structural condition. Since that area was on the fringes, there was much construction going on. Akosua noticed there were many other incomplete or abandoned structures. Some were illegal structures. The local community tried to enforce the weak development controls. However, due to the new-found wealth from the oil economy and the resulting high rate of construction, it was very difficult. As such, the local planning agencies had not kept up with growth in the greater Lagos suburbs.

In areas where development planning lagged behind growth, property owners subdivided the lots themselves and sold them to developers. In such circumstances, it was extremely difficult to control development. A complete subdivision could be developed and built before work actually started on the drawing boards or before local planning agencies initiated a development review process. As a result, illegal structures sprung up on any available empty space, resulting in informal growth. Provision of services thus became a secondary matter, also dependent on the wealth and

48

networking of the developer.

Akosua counted many incomplete blocks in the area. In their L-shaped block, wood and cement blocks were packed in a corner. The place was very quiet. There were two other women in the building. They were from a French-speaking country, Akosua noticed from their accent. They spoke little English; however, Aunt Rose spoke with them in French and a little English. Grace sat and called Akosua to sit by her. Aunt Rose introduced her party to the ladies. They exchanged greetings, smiled, and looked at each other. They were all in their late teens and there was some resemblance. Akosua guessed by the smiles on their faces that they were welcomed.

There were six rooms, a toilet, a bath, and a storage area. Aunt Rose invited Akosua and Grace to her room. Three rooms were used by Aunt Rose, and a room for each of the two ladies. The latter prepared food for Aunt Rose, her niece, and friend. They all sat in the living room and talked that evening about the hustle and bustle in the city of Lagos. Akosua and Grace got the impression they were to look for work the next day. They realized that to pursue their dreams they would have to work very hard and accept any job offered. Aunt Rose also advised them to work very hard at any job they got. They heard stories of other friends and relations who had made it big through hard work and hustle. Akosua had no vocational training and was not sure of the type of work she wanted to do. However, she remained very bold and was prepared for the worst. Her training at home in Ghana had been under very strict and rigid discipline. She was not really used to this type of hustle.

On the other hand, Akosua thought her training at school had been more tailored towards a job with the hope that she could have continued with higher education and qualify to work in an office setting. At this particular stage in her life, she knew nothing except how to read and write English and solve basic math. Songs like "Baa-Baa Black Sheep" and an unrelated syllabus on the sheep and the wool had been given to them at schools in Ghana. She was used to learning and memorizing to write an examination, only to forget the information later. She had also learned songs on winter and snow, even though she had never seen what snow looks like. She could communicate all right, however, she realized there was something missing in her. Her lack of skills and experience in trade or vocational work hampered her ability to meet the challenges ahead. Akosua could not even type.

Grace and Akosua thought about the most interesting opportunities. Options open to them were either as house cleaners or in restaurants as full-time table servers, cleaners, or bartenders. They estimated and compared the options. There was the monetary factor about how much they could earn and save. Yes, Akosua thought very much about savings. She wanted to continue her education. Akosua and Grace then wrote down the priorities in their lives. It was Akosua's wish to work in the city for a year or two and then continue to college to study. The choice of the place for studies was very open. Her preference had always been to study in the United States. She planned to spend a year or two in Lagos where she could start with Community College, or to travel to America to go to college when she passed the required Scholastic Aptitude Test. She knew with determination, perseverance, and dedication, her objectives could be achieved. She was not in a race with anyone.

At night, Akosua thought about Ghana. She wanted to know the story about the runaway girls from Ghana. She knew her father would never understand her. Akosua wanted no control from her parents. Poor parental guidance had made it impossible for her to achieve her ambitions at home. She wanted to rebel because she felt she could not be forced into marriage just for someone else's selfish ends. "I will write to them when I start working," Akosua said to herself.

Her objectives were firmly laid out; she opted to work as a house maid because she could earn a lot of money if she were lucky.

As a live-in house maid, she would save about a hundred to three hundred dollars a month after all expenses. She had been advised it was better to work in a high-income expatriate home rather than one of a local businessman. She ruled out the option of working in a restaurant because the pay was very low and the work was very hard.

About two days later, Aunt Rose came home with a young man. He was to take Akosua to work for a Brazilian couple in one of the most exclusive neighborhoods of Victoria Island, Lagos. Aunt Rose had arranged it without Akosua's knowledge. It was a big surprise to her. Aunt Rose knew the Brazilian family very well. Akosua was to be paid a hundred and fifty dollars per week, or $600 per month, as a live-in maid. The arrangement between Aunt Rose and Akosua was that a percentage of her salary would be paid to Aunt Rose for the first four months to show her gratitude and pay her back for the expenses she incurred on their trip from Ghana to Lagos. She had free food, a room to herself, and a job as a live-in maid twenty-four hours a day in the house.

Aunt Rose told her that the employers were very nice. Aunt Rose then made them aware that she was arranging a job for Grace in another neighborhood. Grace's work and salary were being finalized. Aunt Rose helped pack the few clothes Akosua had brought from Ghana and personally took her to her employers. Akosua was warmly welcomed. There was a cook in the house. She learned he was also from a French-speaking country; however, he spoke English fluently. Communication in the house was in English. Her employers had a good command of the English language. She understood they stayed in Europe for a long time after leaving South America before they came to Lagos.

Akosua started working the following day. There was peace in the household and generally conditions were congenial for making a living. Her duties in the house included babysitting and going on errands for the family. Apart from the newborn baby, there were three children aged three, five, and six. Work in the house was monotonous, but she worked very hard. At times, she felt lonely as the days went by. It was very quiet and was worse during weekdays when they were all at work. On some weekends, she would look after the children when the parents were out of town. She sometimes took them to the park to play or to the library. Akosua usually stayed within the compound of the house because there were not many errands to be run. Her employers were good to her.

On the weekends, a man would come to do the laundry, vacuum the house, mow the lawn and some plumbing work. He worked for a cleaning agency. This man, John, was very hard working. Akosua had not talked to him since she started working except to say hello at times. She had been watching him closely. He looked like a good guy.

The mistress in the house also praised John all the time. Akosua felt a little uneasy about the relationship between the mistress and John. The mistress gave special attention to him in the household when her husband was away. When her husband was at home, the treatment was very different. One day, Akosua overhead the mistress describing her husband's weekly itinerary to John. She was arranging a meeting with John somewhere in the city, but Akosua could not understand exactly what was going on. When the husband was not at home, John had access to almost every place in the house. It was very different when the man was home. Akosua suspected immediately that something was going on between them.

Akosua later learned a lot about what had been happening. Both the husband and the wife were engaged in extramarital affairs. However, the husband did not know there was something going on between John and his wife until he came home unexpectedly one Saturday evening when he was supposed to be away. At that time, the mistress was out in town and did not come home until very late.

That night, Akosua put all the children to bed after reading bedtime stories to them. She laid down on a sofa in the room. There was no one in the house except herself and her employer. She wondered what was happening in the house. She felt sorry for him with the wife out of the house at that time of night. Just as she thought about this, there was a knock at her door. It was the man of the house. He walked over to where Akosua was sitting and they talked about the children. He sat by her. Akosua could read him. The next moment she was in his arms. He made love to Akosua. She consented, mostly out of fear. She was very sacred. It was quiet in the house; the children were fast asleep.

She could hear nothing but the nearby waves from the Atlantic Sea. She could hear dogs barking and she did enjoy that evening. She had not had sex education and was afraid she might get pregnant. The man left and Akosua fell asleep. She did not know what happened in the house later. She did not know when the mistress came home. However, her relationship with the employer became a weekend affair and continued for at least several weeks whenever the woman and the children were not at home. She learned more about sex from this man. From that time on, the man gave Akosua money and other expensive items.

One Saturday when she was off-duty, Grace called and visited Akosua. She had put on weight. She helped Akosua for some time ironing clothes. They then had lunch together. Grace wondered where Akosua had been buying all the expensive handbags and other personal items. Akosua did not disclose anything to Grace. Grace told Akosua she was now employed by a German family. She narrated almost everything that had happened to her since they departed. Her employers, the German couple, had entrusted a lot of household responsibilities to her.

Akosua confessed to being lonely and missing a lot of people dear to her. She did not actually tell Grace about her experience with her employer. Akosua knew Grace would laugh at her and tell the news to her Aunt, so, she kept her lips shut tight. Their conversation centered on their future. Grace said she would work hard for a year, save some money, and go on to continue her studies. She wanted to be a qualified trained nurse. Akosua had thought about her future, too. She had long cherished the ability of speaking several languages and longed to enter the medical profession. Thus, she wished to continue her education and become a medical practitioner or hold some other related medical occupation. Since she had run away from home, she felt she owed it to herself to get a good career in order to be very independent. In the absence of adequate parental care, she had to build her own future.

Akosua later saw Grace off at the gate. She had to rush for a bus. Akosua planned to pay a visit to her place when convenient. The old order in the house continued. It was the same routine work — very interesting, but boring at times. Akosua was lucky, in a way; the new baby was not troublesome at all. She had some peace in her daily work. The other children, however, wanted all the attention. There was some tension in the house. Akosua was dating her employer, and Akosua suspected her mistress was also having an affair. Her mistress called her one morning and gave her some old dresses to put on at home during her household duties. She was pleased with her services. At least the gifts were an expression of her appreciation. That afternoon, her boss called her and asked if she wanted to move to a separate room. Akosua readily accepted the offer because there would be more privacy. The room was furnished with a big-sized television. In the evening, she moved into her private, detached unit after her household duties. Everything happened so fast and seemed so strange.

One day during the week her boss came home before the usual time. His wife was out of town on a business trip. He called Akosua to his guest room. Akosua knew he had something in mind. He told Akosua how beautiful she was and that he appreciated her services very much. The affair with him continued under the most secretive conditions. This went on for some time with no one suspecting. Her boss had been extremely nice to her. He continued giving Akosua expensive gifts and buying her nice clothes. Akosua had second thoughts about the affair, and sometimes became very scared and nervous, especially when her mistress happened to be around. There were times when the woman would look Akosua straight in the eye as if she were sending her a message. This problem made her very unhappy, and she decided to move out immediately if an opportunity came her way.

As she laid on her bed one night in the new room, she had several thoughts. As she looked up at the ceiling, she asked herself several questions. Her mind immediately sent her back to Ghana. She thought of her parents. She thought of what might have happened to her mother. She knew she had no regrets; she owed apologies to no one, but she felt she should at least tell them she was alive. Akosua finally wrote them a letter and sent some money to her parents. Surprisingly, she received a very encouraging letter from her mother some weeks later. She requested Akosua to keep in touch very often and come back home. They were really happy about the money she sent them. Akosua promised herself to send regular remittances to the folks back home and also to the foreign bank accounts she had opened in the United States and England. At least the foreign savings would be enough for her college education. Akosua felt satisfied with herself as the days and weeks went by. She kept the arrangements she had made with Aunt Rose. In fact, she had completed the payments to her. However, she continued to keep in touch as a sign of respect.

The Brazilian family who employed her had almost changed her lifestyle; however, there was hidden tension under the peaceful and cordial relationship. She had good food and everything at her disposal in the house. However, despite all the money and gifts the man gave her, she was not happy with the affair with her employer. Apart from this problem, Akosua knew she wanted more money to increase her savings. She thought this would enable her to buy a ticket to travel and pursue her college education. It was neither greed, nor lust, nor any extravagance; it was a reality of life when she compared herself to other girls who made about three hundred dollars a week in hotels.

CHAPTER 4
Akosua's Career

October, 1988

Akosua had been in the Brazilians' residence for over ten months now. With hard work and their much needed support and affection, she enjoyed living with them in the house. However, she still thought of leaving and seeking employment in a hotel. She wanted the money desperately. She also grew more nervous and worried the more she saw the mistress of the house. She finally mentioned to her boss about leaving the household. He was not surprised, but he did not know exactly what Akosua wanted to do. Akosua's mind was made up. No persuasion could have changed her mind. Akosua gave them three weeks' notice to look for another maid. She had worked hard for them but could tell that the wife was unhappy. Akosua knew all the time that the woman suspected her of having a relationship with her husband, but there was no way to prove it. Her suspicions hung over all interactions. Akosua could tell by the eye contact; it was all over the mistress's face, she *knew*.

Unfortunately for Akosua, on a windy evening, the wife who was annoyed, called her. She openly confronted Akosua of having an affair with her husband. She tried to hit Akosua, but the husband stopped her. There were a few very nasty moments, with arguments between the man and his wife, and chairs flying all over the place. Akosua quickly packed her clothing and other items to leave the household. She picked up her suitcase and said good-bye to her employer. The man hurriedly arranged a ride for Akousa to the bus stop, from a neighbor next door. Not surprisingly, the woman was not in an understanding mood; she was shocked and stared at Akosua as she left the house. The man paid her salary for the remainder of the week. Akosua was dropped at the bus stop by the neighbor, who had been a witness to the marital troubles of the household. It surprised Akosua to know how the wife came to know about her affair with the husband. On the way to the bus stop, the neighbor told her that the wife had hired a private detective who had been following every move the husband made. It was only the night before the confrontation that the wife had got hold of hard evidence on tape.

As if Akosua knew what was about to happen, she made her own arrangements with a girlfriend to move out to the Queens Hotel in the Lagos suburbs. Akosua did not inform Grace nor Aunt Rose about the scandal in the Brazilian household, but she knew Aunt Rose would definitely hear about it. Neither did she inform them about her relocation to the hotel. She was too shy to tell her face to face, so on her way to the bus stop, she wrote a short explanation to Aunt Rose and dropped it in the mail.

She got down at the bus stop where her friend Theresa was waiting to escort her to the hotel. Theresa had been a good friend that Akosua met during her stay with the Brazilian family. Theresa used to live about three blocks away in the same neighborhood. They arrived at the hotel, located on a four-acre lot with many trees. It was really a good hideout.

The bright signs of the hotel were on. It was a nice advertisement, written as "THE QUEENS." Akosua did not deserve to be a queen. The hotel was located adjacent to a newly-developing locality in the southern section of the city. It was a low income, high density area built in 1970. The hotel had twenty-five rooms, and all were occupied by beautiful ladies. The areas surrounding the hotel were characterized by gardens and beautiful landscaping. Akosua had the opportunity to get a room because an occupant had left for another country after a year's stay. Residents paid ten dollars a day as rent, exclusive of utilities and garbage collection. This seemed a matter of survival for Akosua. It implied that she had to work hard to earn more than one hundred and fifty dollars a week to survive.

She had no regrets in these endeavors. Rather, she wondered how life at Queens was going to be. She formally met the other ladies, both black and white, already staying in the hotel. They were of different nationalities. She heard several different languages, from English to French and German to Swahili. Occupants at the hotel could form a small United Nations. Easy communication in English made them socialize promptly. She noticed they were all after one thing — the new economic oil boom in the city. There was understanding, peace, goodwill, and affection. Basically they were in a form of communal living, each with a treasured soul whom they thought could help them make their living and wishes come true.

Each room had a television, a small refrigerator, a toilet, and a bath. The rooms had been beautifully arranged so that privacy was ensured. By all standards, the hotel was a place to relax. The furniture was antique, decent, and simple. What Akosua admired about the hotel was its neatness. The premises were always neat, at least this raised the standards. There was a security guard and a porter at the office. The porter worked as front manager and clerk. Life at Queens was organized. Very few people except the management knew the sort of problems, hustle, and uncertainties residents went through.

Customers, she understood, were of age groups ranging from fifteen to sixty years and over. There was a big lounge and a bar adjacent to a swimming pool on the ground floor. The bar usually opened at nine-thirty each night. Customers and patrons would call on the girls after leaving the bar. Depending on who was making a call, one could be lucky. The minimal fee was twenty dollars a call, if not more than fifteen minutes in duration. This was a strenuous job; however Akosua thought of doing her best carefully to achieve her goal. It was an environment where one could not go out easily in the daytime and avoid eyes watching. Therefore, one must sleep during the daytime and relax the body. Akosua's room was next to Theresa's. The first week was terrible. Being a newcomer, a lot of extra attention was given to her. She had been forewarned by the senior residents. They suggested her intended services would be better provided if she consulted a gynecologist. However, she did not take their advice seriously. She thought she was knowledgeable enough to control and take care of herself.

The seniors had earlier given Akosua an orientation which served as an initiation into the Queens Club. The orientation day was wonderful. No one was supposed to drink alcohol. It was strictly business. Akosua put on a neat dress. Her facial make up was done by a professional hired by the residents themselves. She also rehearsed the code of conduct of the hotel, and more especially of her living condition. The initiation ceremony involved a lecture to newcomers by the "queen mother", the head of all women in Queens Hotel. It centered on maintenance of standards and contribution to a welfare club. There was also a ritual that concluded the orientation ceremony. Akosua recited the code of conduct and promised to respect others, acknowledging that she was not there to prostitute, but rather was there as a victim of a social and economic order. She promised to treat other people with respect and also to have a goal in her life. She finally promised not to make this a permanent job. Finally, she took an oath and signed the code of conduct. She was made to understand that she could easily lose her residency if any of the regulations were broken. At least there was order and enjoyment in the orientation ceremony.

A duty roster was prepared by the clerk at the hotel. There was a weekly rotation of work. The system was very helpful. It was all under the banner of keeping the environment to a standard to benefit the residents. A duty person had to ensure the maintenance of order on the premises. The clerk at Queens was a very strict person. His name was Quayson, and he made sure an inspection was carried out at least once a day. During the hours of inspection of the premises, you were not supposed to entertain visitors. Actually, the hotel premises were closed to visitors between the hours of six to ten in the morning. This was made to give the residents some rest and also to have their quiet hours. The daily inspection was done immediately after these morning hours. Ladies with dirty rooms and untidy corridors were punished. In fact, what Quayson did was submit to the director names of lazy occupants who failed to keep their room and environment clean. They were very strict. An occupant could face a fine or an immediate ejection from her room.

It had been only four weeks at the hotel, however, to Akosua it seemed longer. She had good companions and very good friends. Akosua witnessed an overwhelming rush on her because of her beauty. However, her friend Theresa gave her the secret in the trade. She made Akosua realize that about fifty percent of the men who come there must have some problem with their private life in one way or another. The trick was that Akosua did not have to have sex with all the men who came to her. She simply had to be very smart and perform oral sex and arouse them by touching and caressing. Intercourse was to be the last resort. If it was possible, she should avoid it, because after touching their most sensitive parts, most of the men would be satisfied and she could promise them a second chance after collecting their money.

Sometimes, Akosua regretted some of her actions because she was getting all sorts of customers. The information she gathered early on was that in such a business you could not distinguish between the rich and the poor, nor could you easily identify one who could pay the most. Since it was a money affair, one could not reject even the most ugly and shabby looking man because it might be he who could pay the most. She had been told earlier to collect her fees first and truly she was never found wanting in this. She was always ready to stretch her hands to receive. She had to use a fake identity to the clients due to the fact that she was afraid someone from Ghana might recognize her name. That would have been the end of Akosua in Ghana. She could never return if any clients from Ghana recognized her.

Her first customer on her first business day was a handsome, well-built, healthy-looking fellow called Thomas. Her second customer was a student who requested her to be his girlfriend. He wanted a relationship. Akosua did not bother to chat long with him because she had been warned about students by the seniors at the hotel. They claimed most of the students at the local universities did not have much money, unless the student was one of the sons of the rich oil businessperson in Lagos. She could easily identify the rich students. In these developing countries, about ninety percent of university students used the public transportation. The few who had cars were the sons and daughters of the rich. The poor students were only a headache and might bring problems, instead of giving comfort and happiness. A resident at the hotel could not pay the rent and support herself by following students. This guy from the local university campus was George Lucas. She asked him to leave after collecting the little money he had. Being smart, Akosua did not have sex with the first two clients. She did all that she knew and collected her fee. Her third customer for the night was John, a boxer. He was good looking, but being that it was the first time with him, she did not want to be very receptive. She just collected her money and went about the business as others.

The fourth customer that night was an old man. He was rich by his standards. He stayed a little bit longer and gave her sixty dollars. This guy was very interesting. His tongue was all over her body, and he wanted to enjoy his money to the fullest. She welcomed him to visit again because the old man did not really come for sex. It was the company and the excitement she had when Akosua touched him again. On her first business night, she received

Akosua outsmarts the guys

a hundred and thirty dollars. She was happy with this amount, but was told the amount was really not that much; some lucky occupants could get over two hundred and twenty dollars per night. She felt extremely weak after the first night but knew she would get used to the routine.

Her second day was much worse. She was getting dressed that evening when the director of the hotel himself knocked on her door. He sat down, and said they had a lot to talk about. He said he had just called to welcome Akosua to the hotel as part of his routine informative sessions with new residents. Akosua could not believe when the director proposed to have sex with her. She refused him, though the man thought he had an advantage due to his position in the hotel. Akosua kissed and touched him as she had done to her other clients. Akosua could not collect any fee, but asked him to instruct his clerk that she was not paying rent for a week. He agreed to pay her rent for five days in exchange for the time he spent with Akosua. He later left and promised to look after Akosua during her stay at the hotel. She knew then she could manipulate him. She promised herself not to allow the man into her room again. That was his first and last. Other residents later told Akosua that was how he had welcomed each one of them. They had nothing against him except that he never wanted to pay.

About five minutes after the director left, there was another knock at the door. It was her first customer, Thomas, the good looking guy had come again. As usual, Thomas paid and wanted to stay longer than necessary. Akosua told him he had to pay more if he chose to stay longer. He obliged and even wanted to know more about Akosua. He also asked about the possibility of having regular sessions with her. However, Akosua made him aware that this was strictly business and that she did not want a relationship, if that was what he wanted. He later left.

About thirty minutes later, George Lucas also called. Akosua told him nicely that she was not ready for him. She asked him to leave. Suddenly, the man got mad. He started shouting that Akosua had taken his money before and refused to have sex with him. The noise was unusual, therefore, security was called to take him away. He swore he'd teach Akosua a lesson. He finally left. Later that evening, Akosua had several other clients. She made almost two hundred and eighty dollars on the second night, and she was not having sex with all of them. She did, however, realize the business was very good, but at the same time dangerous. Some of the men became wild if she collected the money but refused to have sex with them. She got tired easily.

Her first client on the third day was named Banson, a businessman living in Lagos. Akosua kept very quiet as he bragged about the nice things he had. She listened and was very good at judging him. He was not smart but he had money. Akosua could be even smarter than him because that was something he should not have mentioned to her about his business. She collected her money and he left when it was all over. Others came in and left. Sometimes it was very difficult to count and even distinguish the customers. However, it was very easy to count the money for the day.

One customer on the third day was an elderly man called Thompson. He was a pensioner from the railways. Akosua was surprised that this old man could be a patron at the hotel. She decided to give this old man a wild time. They spent about twenty minutes negotiating and bargaining based on the time he wanted to spend with her. To Akosua's surprise, the man did not really come for sex but wanted to be massaged, caressed, and touched. He was so happy that he paid her eighty dollars for the time. Akosua took his number and asked him to call and come again as he pleased. Surprisingly, he gave Akosua an extra twenty dollars as he left.

Her next customer was a university student. He was very different. As they talked, she got a call from one of the residents that the person who just entered her room was the son of one of the richest men in the town, and that he was good and very generous.

Akosua outsmarts the guys

by
Rismed avan
Kwasi Basampen

Apparently, they had seen him walk to her room. He had good looks and was very presentable. His name was Femmy. He was so handsome that Akosua could not resist his invitation. He paid her and left upon agreeing on the next suitable date to come and pick her up to go to Akoka University campus.

Her final customer for the day was a big-time lawyer, and a Lagos socialite. He was called Tommy. He claimed he was from Ghana, and that even worsened his case. Realizing this, Akosua gave a false name and refused to have sex with him. The man kissed her and paid her, anyway. The traditional set up of her people at home forbade the job she was doing.

It was the same routine every day during the following weeks at the Queens, but she was saving at least a hundred dollars a day after all expenses. Not bad, she thought. She had several customers of different nationalities from the West African Coast, from Europe, and a few from the Middle East. Others were from the South African region. During these months, business boomed for her. It surprised her, and more especially the older, senior residents. She got more in a day than she could have gotten in a week from the Brazilian family. Upon the advice from some of the senior residents, she planned her savings in such a way that she could send remittances home, buy enough clothes, pay for rent far in advance, and save towards her future travels and college tuition.

She got in touch with Grace and Aunt Rose later to inform them of her new job. Not surprisingly, they were very busy working. Both were professional secretaries in downtown Lagos. Aunt Rose referred to her scandal at the Brazilian residence. She said she laughed and laughed when she got the short note from her. She told Akosua that her former Brazilian employer had been looking for her in the city. Akosua called Aunt Rose regularly, who advised her on her health and the risks involved in this type of work, despite all the money. Upon her insistence, Akosua made appointments to visit a doctor once a month. However, on several occasions she did not honor some of her appointments.

She awoke one weekend to a fine morning. It was this weekend she had an appointment with Femmy, the rich student from the University. The guy looked nice. He had promised to pick up Akosua to take her to their campus dance that night. Upon their arrival at the campus, she noticed that the place was very beautiful. The landscape was planned for an academic environment. However, the university campus's area was limited, and the population density seemed high. It was a congested campus. Her thoughts went far back to the Ghana University campus she visited during her school days. She did not know why her friend Femmy was so popular. Almost every person they passed by on the campus seemed to exchange greetings with him. She realized Femmy felt proud to have her walking by him on the campus. They were yelling and shouting at Femmy all around. They were shouting and calling things such as, "One to one!" "Only you, baby!" "Wow!" "No hustle!" and "For your eyes only."

Her weekend with Femmy was unique because it was the first time she had mixed freely with students from a higher institution in Nigeria. She heard very silly jokes from several students. She did not give her address to anyone on the advice of Femmy. He was jealous and afraid that Akosua would fall in love with someone else on the campus. His fear was based on the work Akosua had been doing at the hotel. Akosua requested Femmy on his last night at the campus to allow her to participate in the free-for-all dancing in the Residence Halls. Students and some elders were all dancing in an open area to a local band. It was termed the "Lowering of Standards" dance. It was more of a rag day celebration where the fraternities allowed the worst behavior for only that occasion. She noticed heavy drinking among the students. However, she was moved by the music, so she got up to dance. Femmy stood up and followed her steps with his hands around her all the time. There were several female students dancing alone.

Later it was all over and Akosua felt satisfied. Femmy gave her a hundred dollars on their way back to the hotel. She realized he was really the son of a rich Lagos socialite. Apart from the money, Femmy promised to pay her rent for the weekend. It was a really small amount, compared with what she would have made had she stayed at the hotel. This was because during the weekend, she could have made hundreds of dollars. She did not care much, though, because she had really enjoyed herself.

Back at the hotel, when she told her weekend experience to some of the others, they started hurling insults at her. They implied she was not serious and that it was not advisable to follow students to their hostels on weekends because they did not have money; she could have been raped by other students in the hostel. They advised her that it was better to go on a weekend with a businessman or someone who was rich.

"They were right," she said to herself. Femmy kept visiting Akosua; however, she refused all invitations to the university campus again. She made sure she restricted and controlled him whenever he was at the hotel.

It had been four months since she first came to the hotel. Akosua had been exchanging letters and telephone calls with Grace and Aunt Rose. She decided to visit them one day. She wrote a letter to Grace and discussed her future plans in the letter. Unexpectedly, about two weeks after she sent the letter, Grace and her Aunt called the hotel. Aunt Rose was not very surprised at Akosua's savings. She said that insofar as Akosua could take care of herself, she didn't care in the least.

Life went on as usual until one day, when Akosua was returning from town, she was attacked by someone. Akosua recognized the face of George Lucas, who wanted his money back because Akosua did not have sex with him. He threw a stone at her. It was in the night and Akosua fell down. He was about to hit her again but stopped upon hearing the sound of people coming to her rescue. Akosua was rushed to the hospital, where she was hospitalized for three days. Following her discharge, Grace called and visited her as often as she could. Akosua started to have second thoughts at the business she was engaged in. She realized how risky it was and how lucky she had been. It was not the same story each day. Akosua stopped meeting different men. Rather, she called the old pensioner, Mr. Thompson. He had called regularly. He loved Akosua, not for sex, but for fun and companionship. Akosua was in a strong relationship with him for a long time until the man moved out of town.

Akosua then remembered Paul, the Peace Corps member she had met during their journey to Lagos. They had several experiences in common. Paul traveled to Lagos via the border. When he arrived at the border with Aunt Rose, Grace, and Akosua; Paul had left them to go to his posting, which was about a hundred miles away in the country. He often came to Lagos, but only on weekends. Akosua wrote to him on several occasions and he replied to all her letters. They continued to exchange letters for some time until Paul planned to come to a festival in Lagos and promised to visit Akosua. Akosua arranged to meet Paul at the local cultural festival. Paul mentioned that during the days he spent at Ghana, he got to know Akosua's parents but did not really know her. During a long discussion over lunch, Akosua joked and asked him whether he passed through the informal bushes at the border. He laughed and said no, however his camera was stolen. He knew so much about the infamous border in Lagos.

After discussing her situation, Paul felt very sorry for Akosua for undertaking her current work in order to save for her future college tuition. Akosua told him how she had come to live at the hotel and the reasons behind it. Paul said she did not need to do that to achieve her future goals in life. He told Akosua about an incident at his village. It happened at the river near the village. Paul had gone to fetch water from the river when the local taps were not running. He was in the water long, when he noticed two crocodiles staring at him. He could not remember when he jumped to the banks of the river and could not describe the time and the speed with which he ran home. He ran as a fast as he could. The two laughed about this for a time. The other incident he told about occured while he was in the city and fell into a manhole which was not covered. He was a simple, nice person, except that his excessive smoking did not sit well with a lot of people. The two liked each other.

Akosua and Paul began to see each other every weekend. He made her realize the implications and seriousness of falling in love with him. It was a problem for both due to the racial differences. Akosua was no longer active at the hotel. They discussed a number of options and other jobs she could have done to earn lots of money without going out with all the millions of men at the hotel. Upon Paul's advice, Akosua looked for a job in the city and at the same time decided to go to the Kings Community College in Lagos to learn how to type and to take a secretarial course. However, she still preferred to stay at the hotel and pay her rent as usual. The basic difference between the two? Paul cared for Akosua. She, on the other hand, realized that she was in love with him.

Suddenly, money became more of a secondary issue to her. Paul become her primary issue. It was very difficult for Akosua because although Paul's concerns were real, other jobs could not support her life, and despite her new job, her savings were going down. Therefore, she sometimes dated other locals for the money. Paul knew this, but there was really nothing he could do to stop her. Akosua understood him, but with much worry and pain. She trusted him because he was the only man who had taken interest in her, inquiring all the time about her education and her future life at the hotel. She had mentioned to Paul that she wanted to go to college and eventually study medicine.

When they started dating and going out, the other girls at the hotel expressed a lot of concern for Akosua because they felt the relationship was heading nowhere. A Peace Corps worker had no stipend to pay for her rent and other bills. The residents were also jealous because of the other work she had taken and the school she was attending. Surprisingly, Akosua did not care in the least about their concerns until later. She had enough savings to continue for about three months. At that time, she wanted Paul so much that all other issues became secondary. Even going out with a white male didn't seem to worry her.

He advised her to continue with classes at the community college in Lagos before making any attempt to apply to a college in the U.S.A. With the local college education and Paul's help, Akosua prepared for her examinations at the college. Now, Akosua worked in the city as a secretary and had stopped all business at the hotel. Paul took Akosua out several times. Akosua paid her rent as usual, but rarely stayed at the hotel any more. Paul helped her in all ways he thought necessary. Surprisingly, Akosua started visiting the library with him almost every weekend. He changed her character and had plans to take her from the hotel, if possible. Paul could not stop her work there in its entirety.

The fact remained that Paul had her respect, just as he respected her. However, he was the only person whose concerns about Akosua were real, but there was not any sexual enjoyment. Akosua dated Paul for a while, yet Paul never attempted to make love to her. He constantly refused to answer any questions on it. It was only the last night before he left the country that he kissed Akosua, but it was only upon her insistence. Paul had to leave the country since his contract ended. He promised to keep in touch with her.

After Paul was gone, Akosua resumed her full-time activities at the hotel. Paul left a lot of household items for her, including a hi-fi, video sets, cameras, cassette tapes, and about fifty video films. Akosua displayed all of them in her room. She was the center of attraction because the two big speakers gave clear sounds. The system provided music for all the hotel, although she made sure she did not disturb others. Theresa and a few other girls often gathered in her room and listen to good music from the eighties.

Her friends liked being in her room and did not want to leave because she gave them good pop as well as soul music. Things that they could not have purchased or listened to in any club in the city. Akosua had forgotten about Femmy and all the other close clients from the times before Paul. However, she soon started making good money again and was prepared to do away with any young boy or old man who wanted to hang onto her for a longer time. She wanted no more serious friendships, though this was very difficult, as she sometimes felt very lonely. Of course, she could have had a relationship with a nicer guy for a fortnight, provided he was rich. She thought of finding a poster to place on her wall which would have read "STRICTLY BUSINESS". It was lucrative at this time because men were coming to her at the hotel all the time. While in the business, she kept dreaming and thinking about Paul.

The director of the Queens suggested a video club be formed at the hotel using the films Paul left with Akosua. She was to be paid a commission when her videos and other equipment were used. Akosua requested a short term contract to work part-time at the club, to which the director agreed. Most of the films left by Paul were then being shown to the public at the hotel. The hotel became more popular as more and more customers were attracted to the videos and the bar. It was also cheaper to be at the Queens Hotel than most other clubs, at least in the city. Indirectly, some of the ladies experienced a higher rate of patronage from different people from all parts of the city. Because of the success of the video club, Akosua struck a close relationship with the director. It was a good business experience.

She became more conscious of the surroundings of the hotel, the lawns, and the flowers that made the place beautiful. There was adequate landscaping on the lawns. With cooperation from the director, Akosua planted flowers, had the landscape replanted with new grass, and encouraged the residents to undertake regular voluntary cleaning of the premises. Due to their efforts, the compound became very neat and beautiful. The lawns were better kept and the gardens had nice flowers. Almost everyone was doing good business and saving about three hundred and fifty dollars a week.

Akosua had not heard from Paul since he left. Other ladies in the hotel teased her at times because Paul had not written to her. This had a big effect on her. She finally thought about finding a new boyfriend as a companion, a regular one who at times could be a source of inspiration and protection if possible, but not for any serious sexual relationship. As she sat down at times to collect herself and think about her plans for the future, she panicked at the list of men she had entertained at the hotel. The list was endless. She remembered Thomas, George Lucas, John the boxer, Banson, Thompson, and Femmy, not even listing the others who came in for short periods and left

She would have liked to stop all these entertainments and have a constant and permanent companion. Paul would have been the perfect one, but he was gone. There was really no one to confide in. She could not really count on or trust her hotel companions because the girls became jealous of each other quickly. At times she was confused, not knowing what to do. She wanted someone she could trust at all times, provided the love was there. Akosua checked her mail regularly, hoping fort a letter from Paul. She was taking care of her life. She was employed at the hotel; she had a permanent job as a secretary in the city and was studying at the Community College. She did not need all the men any more. However, she decided to take on a permanent boyfriend to while away the time.

She started dating a guy by the name of Lawal who worked as a chef in one of the other big international hotels in town, the Lords Restaurant. Lawal had been working there for the past six years. She got to know Lawal when a guy called Wizzy, a casual friend, took her to the Lords, a nightclub in Lagos. It was a memorable evening. It was there that Lawal approached her, saying he had seen her at the Queens on a particular occasion. Akosua refuted his claims, although Lawal mentioned names of her colleagues. She knew then that he was telling the truth; however, she had to deny his claim on purpose. Lawal asked to see her later knowing that she had company.

The reason she dated Lawal was because with him, she always had a free meal. Akosua had the opportunity to taste several new dishes. Lawal was always giving her food at the Lords Restaurant. Sometimes Lawal would deliver lunch to her at work. Other times, he would pay for Chinese food to be delivered to her at the hotel. He ran errands for her and picked up her prescription drugs when she needed them. Akosua really did not love him, though, because she knew he had been spending time with other women in the city. He used to boast to other men about the many women he had been dating. Akosua loved his food, services, and money. Lawal gave her rides when she was in need and later started buying her expensive clothing. Akosua began to wonder where Lawal was getting all the money. It was strange that Lawal was not even a regular at the hotel. He was too busy a man. Lawal, however, took Akosua to the nicest places in town. It was the same outing almost every weekend when he was off duty. They went to restaurants, concerts, and fashion shows. Unfortunately, he never asked about her or her life, or anything about her in particular. He was a man of instant gratification, born to enjoy life every minute. To him, the future would take care of itself.

Lawal was fond of Akosua. He was proud to have a beautiful girl like Akosua to walk with him in high places. Once when they visited the show grounds, Lawal discussed the possibility of buying out her video club at the Queens so he could start a new video club at the Lords. Akosua thought that was a very silly proposal. She refused to discuss it again any time he brought the matter up. Such a proposal to the director at the Queens would have been very insulting. Akosua brushed the issue aside since that would have been her end at the Queens hotel. As strong in spirit and determined as she was, no one, or more especially no selfish or self-seeking guy, would change her plans or arrangements at the hotel.

They went to a trade fair at the show grounds one day, and Lawal brought up the subject of the video club again. She told him off and asked him to talk about more interesting stories. They walked around the show grounds watching displays of products from several companies from the Western World, Europe and the Far East. Lawal bought her presents at the show grounds, and they ate all kinds of appetizing dishes. The fair at the show grounds was an exhibition of local crafts and modern technological products from other countries. The function was an annual affair, she gathered, with the aim of bringing manufacturers together to establish contacts, show products, and improve upon trade with other people of the world. There were several booths for the entertainment industry. There were live local and western bands. The booths for the breweries were especially full of visitors. Beer and other popular soft drinks were free. Akosua could not count the number of people in the beer hall. The concentration of people was like a high school football stadium at full capacity.

Lawal made her feel very happy on this day. One thing she did realize about Lawal was that he always wanted to impress her by giving her presents either in cash or in kind. He told her several times he was in love with her, although Akosua knew he never wanted to introduce her to other people because of her past life at the hotel. She had failed to inform Lawal that their friendship was just temporary and for her convenience. Akosua asked him later that day to take her back to the Queens. In her mind, she thought that although he was nice, he had really overdone it. His impressions were very superfluous without any real love in them. At times, she stood up to him and challenged him on issues. She stopped following his wishes, as he always had his way around her. He never liked that idea, but there was nothing he could have done.

The following day, there were questions from her mates regarding Lawal. Even Quayson, the clerk, and the director asked her about him. None ever said anything good about him. Akosua knew herself it was the end of her relationship with Lawal. Most of the girls at the Queens had not been as lucky as she was. She was nice to people. This distinguished her from others.

She had been at the Queens over a year now, and she knew that all eyeshad been on her during that time. She had almost every material thing in this world that a woman by her standards was supposed to have. Her savings were high. However, there was pain in her life. It seemed as if she was being haunted by a problem she could not articulate or really understand.

One morning at the hotel, Quayson knocked on Akosua's door. She was already up from bed and tidying her room. Quayson said hi and wondered where she had been all these days. As usual, he requested to be given something good that she must have brought back from town. He wanted either a new cassette tape, biscuits, or even leftovers in her refrigerator. Akosua gave him some biscuits. He, in turn, gave her messages and some letters. There was a letter from her friend, Paul.

"A good guy, really," she said to herself, "one who does not forget a loved one." She also had replies to most of the letters she had written earlier to her parents at Ghana. Her parents had acknowledged other remittances and things she had sent them. Akosua almost froze with joy when she opened the letter from Paul. He had sent his picture and that made her day. He had written from California inquiring about her plans, health, and everything at the Queens. In the letter, Paul remarked about the hospitality he had received in Africa and all the nice people he had met. He missed all the good people he left behind. He wrote about the orientation lectures he had been giving to the students in colleges about Africa.

Paul raised an issue in his letter pertaining to Akosua's stay at the hotel and the possible negative impact it could have on her character. Although Akosua had stopped seeing Lawal and had a good job in the city; she continued to work part-time at the hotel. In addition, she was in the process of completing her studies at the Community College. She was doing very well by all standards. However, she realized Paul was concerned about the possible temptations of seeing men all the time. Akosua thought about it and vowed to do the best she could to avoid any temptations.

She was not desperate for money now because she was financially stable. She set a goal for herself to spend her time wisely on her two jobs and also on her studies. She became much more reclusive at the hotel. She limited the time she spent with other girls who had become very jealous of her because of her two jobs and her refusal to entertain men at the hotel again.

It was on a Tuesday that she got the letter from Paul. For four days, she kept to herself. It was a big change in her life. She turned away all visitors, especially the men who knocked on her door. She did not receive patrons, but spent most time indoors. All her friends and the management thought she was not very happy. They kept asking her questions every day in an effort to find out what was wrong with her. Akosua approached the director of the hotel and discussed with him a possible change of room. She preferred a room further away from the other girls where she thought she would not be disturbed by men. She told the director that she wanted to be very serious in her studies. She had even contemplated the possibility of moving away from the hotel altogether; however, that would have meant the loss of the temporary part-time job she had at the hotel. Also, she would not have had the free rent she was enjoying at the hotel. The director agreed with her and gave her another room at the hotel. Akosua felt good about herself. She tried to be nice to the other girls at the hotel during the little free time she allowed herself.

On the other hand, some of the girls had become cold toward

her out of envy. It was safer to keep quiet and a "low profile" during that time because she did not know who her enemies were. Of course, she could not have ruled anyone out. The girls were all hustling, and jealousy prevailed among them as individuals, or groups, or where there was any social interaction. Akosua wrote a reply to Paul of the positive steps she had made in her life, and later talked to Paul on the phone. Paul encouraged her to keep her spirit and faith very strong and keep her hope and determination high. Paul also reminded Akosua to turn to the Lord and start praying, and if possible, to start going to church.

When Akosua completed her studies at the Community College, she felt it was appropriate for her to leave Lagos. She had not had any sufficient sleep since she got Paul's letter. She thought about Paul all the time, but failed to understand why Paul liked her but refrained from loving her. She asked herself several questions about this all the time, although Paul was gone. Her thought was that Paul must have been turned off by all the men she had entertained before. Akosua continued her work at Lagos and tried her best to achieve her goals in life until one day the unexpected happened.

CHAPTER 5
Akosua's Rewards and a Final Sojourn

January, 1989

On a bright Wednesday morning, Akosua heard other girls and residents at the hotel shouting. She heard noises and noticed everyone was running helter-skelter, jumping over tables and beds, screaming and yelling. "Why? What's happening?!" she inquired from the room next door.

"The police have come to the Queens to arrest all the girls," she was told. It was really a police raid on many brothels in the city. She quickly put on her shoes and ran as fast as she could, but to no avail. The police were all over the building. The main gate and entrance were locked.

"All of us arrested?" she asked herself. The arrest was the most brutal scene Akosua had ever witnessed in her life. The police kicked the girls who resisted arrest. Just as Akosua was about to reach the stairs, she ran into two policemen. She told them she was a hotel employee, not a prostitute. The policemen did not listen. With force, they tried to push Akosua into her room. Akosua became very disturbed and wild, thinking the policemen wanted to rape her. She struggled with them but was not that strong; however, during the struggle, a policeman tried to tear off her dress. Akosua got mad and with all the force she gathered, freed herself from the police and ran as fast she could towards a window. Thinking the level from the window was low, Akosua jumped. She fell from a second floor window. She was rushed to the hospital and was admitted. Luckily, her injuries were not that severe.

Her close friends, including Grace and Aunt Rose, heard about her case and visited her at the hospital. They were there most of the time. The other girls were taken to the police station. They were packed into a police truck which was very dirty and smelled bad. There was absolute darkness in the truck. It was called the "Black Maria." They never understood why it was given that name. You could tell it had not been washed or cleaned for months. This was a truck used to convey prisoners. The girls were not prison inmates in the real sense; however, once they were arrested they were treated as prisoners.

It was noisy when they arrived at the police station. They were lined up and their names taken. They numbered about twenty. The police requested to see the resident permits that allowed the girls to stay and work in the country. None of them had any work permit. The management at the hotel had told the girls that everything was fine, and they were not to worry about permits. The hotel and the resident girls had taken advantage in the laxity of laws and the permissiveness in the society. The girls wondered why they were being arrested despite the fact that there were many other brothels in the area. Most of them did not even know the brothels were illegal in the city because they had had police and military personnel as clients, yet none of them had complained or questioned them. They were all surprised.

With all the oil wealth in the city, many of these resident hotels had sprung up all over the place. The inspector said he was waiting for the hotel director to come by so that he could arrest him too. The director, as he was fondly called at the hotel, called some minutes after. He waved at them and whispered that everything would be all right. He went straight to the office of the police commander. Surprisingly, a little while later they were all released on bail, but with several conditions. They were to obey the laws in the city and refrain from any indecent act. They were made to sign a statement to be on good behavior. They were informed about Akosua being admitted at the hospital. The director told the police commander that one of his employees had been admitted to the hospital because she had tried to run away from police harassment. The commander promised an investigation into the matter. On their way back to the hotel, they all stopped at the hospital to visit Akosua. They learned that her injuries were not serious. The doctor said she would be there for two weeks.

That night all the girls met at the conference room in the hotel. The director requested their presence for a small meeting. The hotel was closed to customers that night. The director told them this was not an unusual arrest, but that this type of thing had been going on for years. The hotel had been late in paying a patronage fee to the peace officers, which though illegal, was normally done to protect a business. He said these raids were not common when a payment was late or had not been paid. This particular raid was the second one in four years. His advice to them was to be calm. It was obvious that most of the residents were foreigners from the west coast. Most of them had no traveling documents, let alone residence permits. The director and Quayson left, and the girls organized their own meeting. Among other suggestions at the meeting was that there should be a donation of about ten dollars from each resident every month. The donation would go to a welfare or charitable society in Lagos in the name of the hotel management. Over three hundred dollars was later collected and given to the director, who in turn sent the donation to the Association of the Wives of Peace Officers. Most of the girls were very worried about the donation, or more specifically, the recipients, because their gesture could have backfired on them. However, the hotel management asked them not to worry. They prayed for Akosua's quick recovery. At this time most of them felt that Akosua legally was not one of them, however, they all shared sympathy for her. They sent her flowers.

The encounter with the police had given Akosua a lot of concern. Lest she forget, it was not her first encounter with the police. One evening, she had gone out with Paul before his departure. They went to watch a film, then danced the night away at a club. They forgot there was a curfew in the city and that they should have been carrying a curfew permit. They had none, and the police arrested them on their way back home. It was another experience she did not want to forget. The police released them.

Akosua was discharged from the hospital, and Aunt Rose and Grace accompanied her back to the hotel. There was a surprise party at the hotel for her return. She was still in pain and had been asked to schedule several follow up check-ups and therapy sessions. It was an opportune time for Akosua to evaluate herself and her stay at the hotel. She really wanted to leave at the earliest possible opportunity; however, she had to fulfill some of her obligations first. She had a paper to write at the college, and she also wanted to complete her contract jobs, both at the hotel and in the city. Not surprisingly, two ladies left for another hotel of their own accord. Others planned to make packing a gradual process.

"But where do they go?" Akosua asked herself. "Do they have to move to another hotel?" She thought that was unnecessary because there would be the same problems at other establishments. The infrequent police raids would continue. Every hotel in the area would be harassed one after another. The truth was that although the local government had made prostitution itself illegal, not a single local authority had made any conscious effort to enforce the law. Those who set the laws and others who enforced the laws were themselves customers at the hotels. The leaders and decision makers in the society were much more concerned with making money from the oil boom and had no time to waste on arresting prostitutes. Also, just as in other developing societies, laws were fine on paper; the implementation, however, left much to be desired. This was due to the fact that the social structure and the organization of local communities were that of a linked, extended family and networks of relationships. One would not be surprised to find that some local government authorities had invested in brothels and disguised them as hotels since it was a very lucrative venture. Enforcement of the laws, therefore, often meant hurting and trampling upon personal interests and relations. Secondly, the growth in population had stretched and exceeded the number and capacity of police offices in the city. Most hotels took advantage of these laws.

The director pleaded with all the other girls to stay at the hotel. Their presence in the hotel enhanced his business. Aunt Rose and Grace visited Akosua at the hotel while she was still recuperating from her wounds. Akosua, after discussions with Aunt Rose, formally approached the director of the hotel. Their case was that Akosua was an employee at the hotel and that she was almost raped by the policemen. In the course of the struggle, she had hurt herself. They planned to hire a lawyer to sue both the hotel management and the police commander. The director was surprised; however, after some thought, he later called Akosua and Aunt Rose and pleaded with them not to go on with the case. Rather, the hotel would help in Akosua's rehabilitation and pay her an undisclosed amount of money for the time she was absent from work and her studies. Part of the arrangement was to provide a specialist for Akosua to undergo several x-ray and tests to find out if any internal damage had been done.

Akosua wrote to Paul in detail about the incident and her recuperation and Paul replied and urged Akosua to leave the hotel immediately and stop that work all together. It was either that, go back to Ghana, or get into college. He really wanted her to find some other work. However, after discussions with Aunt Rose, Akosua realized she had much unfinished business before she could leave. She wrote in detail explaining her time, college, work, and hospital check-ups to Paul. She made him aware that she would definitely leave the hotel at the earliest possible time.

Akosua's rehabilitation continued. She regularly visited a private clinic on Kenny Street. Upon each visit, the hotel provided a taxi to take her to and from the clinic. The doctor gave her some drugs and an injection and requested to see her again in four days. At times, she did not know what was happening to her, and she would experience severe pain.

She went to another clinic four days later. This time she was made to stay longer for a thorough check-up. After several laboratory tests, the doctor called her and said her recovery might take longer than they thought. Akosua asked the doctor to put that in writing to the hotel management. The doctor referred Akosua to a specialist. The implication of the need for a specialist showed her that her injuires were very serious and needed urgent attention. Fortunately, she got an appointment with a specialist later on.

On the day of the appointment, she spent almost an hour at the clinic. There was a delay as the specialist had an urgent call to surgery. Akosua had another x-ray, tests and a physical. She later returned to the hotel. As the taxi got closer to the hotel, she noticed a crowd, heard noises, and the voices of Quayson, the director, and others laughing and joking at the front gate. She did not use the main entrance to the Queens, but used a side entrance to her room instead. There were no messages. She then locked the door, took some of the prescribed medicine, and went to bed. She was disturbed by knocks on the door several times, but she had earlier vowed not to open it to anyone that day. It was time to take stock of her activities at the Queens, or at least to have a sober reflection of herself. Appointments with the specialist were her main concern.

Not a week passed without a visit to the clinic. She went to the specialist yet again, this time for the results of other tests. This was very surprising because up to this time the specialist had not been able to determine the cause of the severe pains she had been having, nor whether she had broken any bones during her fall. During this time Akosua was paid by the hotel for her part-time job although she was on an extended leave of absence. She was also lucky to be given a paid leave of absence from her other job in the city. However, she had a very short time to prepare for her SAT examinations at the Community College. Thus, she had to spend her time between healing, learning, and putting her life back together. As her pain began to lessen and her injuries to heal, her visits to the specialist were farther apart. She was getting better and better. Support from Aunt Rose, Grace, and Paul made her recover very quickly.

Akosua resumed her part-time work organizing the video club at the hotel, and later fully resumed her part-time work in the city. On her return to a full and normal life, everybody welcomed her with open arms and gifts. She spent most of her time in between jobs preparing for the SAT examinations. The day she took the SAT was unlike any other exams she had taken in the past; she was prepared and had matured in her thoughts. She came back from the examination hall expecting high scores.

During this time, Akosua was thinking about leaving Lagos. She had been discussing with Paul the possibility of admission to a college in the United States. Paul was prepared to help her. Not surprisingly, he was happy for Akosua and sent her an invitation letter. He had earlier prompted her to apply to a college in the area where he was living in the United States. Paul had made it very clear to Akosua that he was eager to help her achieve her dreams. He was not interested in love or marital affairs. However, Akosua wanted more from him than that. She really thought as time went by that Paul would change his mind. Paul took his time to write and explained to Akosua the immigration issues in the United States.

Akosua knew she had to leave. She spent most of the time packing and making arrangements to leave the city altogether. The police action at the hotel had compounded her personal problems.

She did not spend any of her savings in Lagos for any unnecessary items. She made sure to economize on what items she did buy. Her total savings stood at six thousand dollars. This did not include the payment made by the hotel for the assault and casualty suffered during the police raid. It also excluded the value of all her personal belongings and those the hotel was still using at the video club.

Now, most of the residents at the Queens could tell Akosua was a different person who had put her life back together. Some weeks later, Quayson called her, "Akosua, Akosua!"

"Come in, Quayson," she replied. As usual, he brought her several letters and messages. There were notes from Lawal, Wizzy, and a host of greetings from several unrecognized people who must have heard of her tragedy. They were all wishing her the best of luck and a speedy recovery. Their letters had come late, though she appreciated the thought.

"Are you still afraid of the police?" Quayson asked. "You look very worried," he continued.

"Yes, and I am still considering whether I should continue to stay at this place or not," Akosua replied.

Quayson thought it was the police harassment that had made her worried, or that she was sick. Quayson, not knowing about her plans, went back to the office and informed the director. The director called Akosua to his office to be sure she had no more problems. He advised Akosua to put all fears away and that the police would not come to the hotel again.

Some months later, she got the results from the SAT test. Akosua exclaimed with joy upon reading the results. She had very high SAT scores. She told herself that this was the time to leave and travel to America to meet Paul. She forwarded the results to Paul, who sent them with her admission package to the Community College she had chosen. With Paul's assistance, the admission procedures to the college in the United States were finalized.

Back at the hotel, Akosua started preparations to leave. She informed the director upon the instructions of Paul and terminated the working contracts she had with the hotel. Actually, her plan was to go back to Ghana, leave her things to her family, and then travel to America to study. She made telephone calls to some friends she knew in London to send her invitation letters so she could visit them in transit. She talked to Paul more often. Finally, the date of her departure from the hotel was near. The director, after accepting her request to leave, wanted to plan a party for her, which she refused. The director was really hurt by Akosua's departure, although she could not say the same was true of the other girls.

On the date of her departure, she signed off from the hotel residence. The director and Quayson came to see her off. Aunt Rose, Grace, Theresa, her close relatives and a few friends came to see her off, as well. Akosua rented a truck which ran a moving service between Nigeria and Ghana. The truck came to the Queens and loaded all her items. She said good-bye to all her friends at Lagos and left with joy and pain at the same time. Her departure suddenly turned into something she did not expect. There were a few girls and friends in the area almost in tears. She was sad but was happy to leave with much excitement about the future. She realized her adventure in Lagos was over. The journey back to Ghana was not as tedious as she had witnessed some years ago.

Back at home in Ghana, Akosua was given a huge reception by her parents. They were very welcoming. Her people and family accepted her with wide open arms. Due to the frequent remittances she made to them, Mr. and Mrs. Mensah were very happy to see her return with all the material possessions. She carried about ten suitcases of clothing, not counting the boxes of shoes and other items. Her folks at home were very materialistic. Since she brought a lot of items and clothing to them, her mother was in the best of moods. Apart from that, Akosua had matured, and her mother talked to her politely. They had forgotten that she had run away from home. Her father was especially impressed, first by the number of gifts given to him, and then by the amount of money she gave to the family. There was a big party for her at home, although Akosua had to finance everything. She still knew she had a future.

Akosua spent a month at home, then bought a ticket and left the country. Her expectations of meeting Paul again and starting a whole new life were high. She left for the United States after a brief stop in London. Upon her arrival in the United States, Akosua first stayed with an old family friend in the mountain states. It was in the month of December. The winter was very severe. On her day of arrival, the area had just had one of their worst snowstorms — about seventeen inches of snow. Can you imagine! It was the first time she shad seen snow, although she had learned about it in Ghana almost fourteen years ago. She had been made to memorize songs about snow, but did not see it until she was almost twenty years old! Akosua still knew how to sing the old songs about snow. She was curious, but not that amazed.

Her visit in the mountain states was just a stop over. There was an old family friend of Mr. Mensah who had been living in the United States for many years. This friend had learned about Akosua's sudden departure from Ghana when he visited one holiday. Akosua started communicating with him through her mother. Her itinerary was to stay with this family friend for a few days before moving on to join Paul in Los Angeles. During her flight to the mountain states, Akosua also experienced a lot of turbulence in flight. Above forty thousand feet from the ground, the airplane started rattling in mid-air, and she was almost tossed from her seat. Her stomach started trembling, and her body was shaken. She was scared.

From the mountain states, Akosua joined Paul in Los Angeles. Paul welcomed Akosua with some friends at the airport. She was very happy to see Paul again. He had grown a beard and had put on much weight since he left Africa. Paul allowed Akosua to stay with him for some time. Although they were not romantically involved, they lived together and did everything as lovers, except make love. It was not very surprising to her that Paul had no interest in women. It was not only Akosua, but he was really not interested in women altogether. He never dated anyone and had no girlfriend. Akosua became a little bit suspicious of him and was afraid he might be dating men. She was not against him being gay; assuming he was, however, Akosua had not been exposed to that kind of life.

During her first weeks in the States, Paul accompanied Akosua to the campus where she was to enroll. On their way, Paul introduced Akosua to an old friend, a woman. Akosua shook her hand by scratching her palm as was the custom in her hometown in Ghana. Surprisingly, the woman later told Paul that Akosua might be a lesbian because she thought Akosua might have been making a pass at her. It made her feel very bad. Paul took time to explain to Akosua about the controversial issues on gays and lesbians in the United States. Akosua contacted the lady and they later became very good friends, just to prove to her that she was trying to be nice. The greeting was the cordial gesture she used to do in Africa with her friends. When this issue came up, Akosua wanted Paul to prove that he was not one of them; she tried the best she could to go to bed with him, but Paul refused. The slept in separate bedrooms. He finally made it very clear to Akosua that he did not mind helping her get settled, however, he was not interested in romance at all and that she had best forget any wishes of romantic involvement with him. Akosua took his word, and they became the best of friends.

During the first few weeks after her arrival, another incident happened at their apartment that made Akosua nervous any time she walked through the streets in the neighborhood. One day when Paul had already gone to school, Akosua washed one of her nice dresses and went out to the roof top to hang the dress to dry in the sun. Unfortunately, there was bang, and the door to the roof top closed with the force of the wind. The door to their apartment was not closed, and she even had the iron on. Leaning over the wall, she tried to get some attention from people on the street seven stories below. Akosua heard shouts from some elderly women, pleading with her not to jump. She was scared and did not know what was going on. She became more and more confused, when suddenly, the ambulance service from the rescue squad arrived. Some talked to her from below while others came up to rescue her. It was very strange. Akosua did not know the elderly women had telephoned the police and told them someone was about to commit suicide by jumping off the roof. When she explained herself to the rescue team, they laughed, understood, and let her go. She was so embarrassed that for three days she refused to go into the streets. Residents pointed anytime she walked down the street. Paul laughed, but sympathized with her when he came home that night.

Some weeks after her arrival, she finalized her enrollment at the community college, and began working as a maid in one of the suburbs. Her employers were Jewish and had migrated from South Africa. They were very strict with her. She had to conform to their wishes and work according to the schedule prepared for her. She was paid two hundred dollars a week, which did not include room and board. The work usually involved picking up the couple's son from school, which was within walking distance, at two o'clock each afternoon, then caring for the boy until his parents returned from work.

Her work schedule was from 2 p.m. to 7 p.m. each day, except for weekends. It reminded her of the experience with the Brazilian couple back in Nigeria. However, Akosua had learned her lesson and swore never to repeat it.

Although she was with Paul, she found life in the United States very strange. People were too individualistic. There was very little togetherness; it seemed as if each person had to care for him or herself. This issue was initially irrelevant and of no concern to her; however, as time went by, she felt very lonely, except the few times she and Paul went out to dinner and attended functions together. Paul himself was very busy. He was trying to complete his graduate program and had two part-time jobs — one in the library on his campus, and also as a pizza delivery person. Akosua was very serious about her studies. Every morning at seven o'clock, she got up and took the bus to the college campus. Her lectures started at half past eight and lasted till mid-day. She then went to her job with the Jewish family.

The college had almost five thousand students, excluding the non-resident student population. Akosua was surprised by a number of issues on campus. Black American students had a society that was very different from the African students' society. There were so many societies based on ethnicity and race that Akosua failed to understand them all. She had expected the African student population to be a part of the Black American society. She also expected the Asian students to be the voice for all Asian students; however, there were several ethnic grouping within all the student unions. Her greatest concern was the division among the Black American and African students. The more she tried to make friends, the more she realized how difficult it was. She did not know whether it was because of her very dark complexion, or because she was from Africa, or both. She did not know whether or not her complexion was the silent, yet major, factor. Akosua realized that even some of the Africans and African-Americans looked down at her because of her dark complexion; as if she had been brought in from a charcoal field. This was a big surprise to her. She felt very lonely on campus. She tried to be friendly with several groups of black females from various ethnic backgrounds, but always got strange looks from them. No one was prepared to spend time with her.

It seemed everyone was either busy doing his or her homework or leaving to go to work. It became very obvious to her that this society was driven by the economic trends of the day. Almost everyone she saw or met was busy working very hard to make ends meet. It took her a long time to read and understand

American history. She realized that blacks in the society had been shaped by the American culture — they were not African at all. The few Africans she met had also forgotten where they had come from. The rapid technological advancement of the white man and the distant separation of the Americas from the African continent had a major impact on the people of African descent.

It took her a long time to understand that there were basic cultural differences between the Africans in Africa, the Africans in the United States, and the African-Americans. It took her even longer to realize that life in the United States was different than life in Europe, and even more different than the lesser-developed countries in Africa. Coming from Africa, she had been shaped by that culture in her dressing and eating habits, in her language and communication, in her attitude to life in general. At first, she blamed everyone around her. She blamed them because they were not interested in her and her affairs. She blamed people any time they told her they were too busy to listen to her. It took her some time before she adjusted to the American way of life.

Akosua's whole life changed for the better during her college days as she began to understand what life was all about, and learned right from wrong in this society. The tough life experiences she had made her a very serious student. During her four years at college, she was totally transformed. She realized she was becoming more of an American than an African. Her dressing changed; her food tastes changed; so did her communication and language. She had little time for other people. She yelled at people in traffic. She worked two part-time jobs with all the seriousness she could muster, just to pay her bills. Although she was attending an inter-denominational Christian church, it was not on a regular basis. She felt sorry for herself when she looked back. She finally realized that people are shaped by the society they live in. There was no need to blame people now. She understood where people came from and also understood their actions. She became much like a black living the

American dream when she graduated with a degree in Biostatistics after four years of college. She forgave her parents for their neglect and the troubles she had gone through. They lived in an old world.

Although, things have changed, it is Akosua's wish that parents give their daughters the best they can to make their education a top priority. She realizes the path she took to make the American dream a reality was not the best; however, she would not want any girl to experience what she did in Lagos. Akosua promises to narrate her life in America in detail in her next short story. Her advice to parents all over the world is that they should give the best education to their teenage girls, and do away with arranged or forced marriages. These marriages often make young women run away and undertake risky adventures. Parents should sacrifice and provide for their daughters. Akosua has learned from her experience. Now that she *is* somebody, she has confessed her past so teenage girls can learn from her mistakes.

The sojourns of Akosua Sojourner Mensah

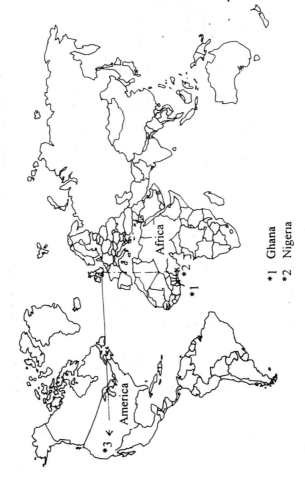

Africa

America

*3 ←

*1 Ghana
*2 Nigeria

Confessions of a Neglected African Daughter

REORDER SLIP

PRDC	

To place an order, please fill out this slip and return
with payment to the address provided.
Please send orders to:

↓

PRDC PUBLISHING
P.O.BOX 3369
WOODMOOR BRANCH
SILVER SPRING MD 20918

Discount of 20% with this order form

(PLEASE PRINT)

NAME_____

ADDRESS _____

CITY _____

STATE _____ **ZIP CODE** _____

BOOK TOTAL   **QUANTITY**_____
$_____

POSTAGE ($1.95 per book, 80 cents each additional book)
$_____

                                        Price/Book: $9.60
TOTAL   Tax :   .40
$_____

                                        Total: $10.00

"
CONFESSIONS OF A NEGLECTED AFRICAN DAUGHTER"